ADDICTIONS FROM AN
ATTACHMENT PERSPECTIVE

The John Bowlby Memorial Conference Monographs Series

ADDICTIONS FROM AN ATTACHMENT PERSPECTIVE

Do Broken Bonds and Early Trauma Lead to Addictive Behaviours?

THE JOHN BOWLBY MEMORIAL
CONFERENCE MONOGRAPH 2013

Edited by
Richard Gill

The John Bowlby Memorial Conference Monographs
Series Editor: Kate White

Routledge
Taylor & Francis Group

LONDON AND NEW YORK

First published 2014 by
Karnac Books Ltd.

Published 2018 by Routledge
2 Park Square, Milton Park, Abingdon, Oxon OX14 4RN
52 Vanderbilt Avenue, New York, NY 10017, USA

Routledge is an imprint of the Taylor & Francis Group, an informa business

British Library Cataloguing in Publication Data

A C.I.P. for this book is available from the British Library

ISBN-13: 9781782201076 (pbk)

Typeset by V Publishing Solutions Pvt Ltd., Chennai, India

CONTENTS

v

ACKNOWLEDGEMENTS

Thanks to The John Bowlby Memorial Conference 2013 Planning Group: Catherine Mitson, Carol Tobin, France Couelle, Helene Everitt, and Brenda Prince for their creative work in producing this conference with the aim of providing some necessary understanding of why addiction is so prevalent in contemporary society. A special thank you to all the contributors to the conference whose knowledge was shared in such a personal way in order to ground addiction in a place of understanding.

The clinicians who presented the paper at the memorial lecture would like to thank their clients for the personal information they generously provided and whose names have been changed to protect their identity.

Finally, thanks to our twentieth John Bowlby Memorial Lecturer, Edward Kahntzian whose courageous work over many years provided a stimulating presentation to open up this conference.

A special thank you to Oliver Rathbone for his continuing belief in the value of publishing these monographs and to Rod Tweedy and his team from Karnac Books for their patience and support in its production and publication.

Permission

In Chapter Four, the excerpt from *Attachment and Loss, Volumes 1 and 2* by John Bowlby (1973) was reproduced by kind permission of The Random House Group.

ABOUT THE EDITOR AND CONTRIBUTORS

Cara Crossan is a qualified and accredited addiction therapist, consultant, and clinical supervisor. She has over thirteen years experience of working with individuals and families affected by addiction. She holds a Masters Degree in Addiction Psychology and Counselling and is a qualified Hazelden trained addiction therapist. Cara specialises in the treatment of trauma and its manifestations in addictions and compulsive behaviours. She has accomplished extensive training with Dr Patrick Carnes and Dr Kenneth Adams in the United States where she is a Certified Sex Addiction Therapist Candidate (CSAT). In the UK, Cara is a trustee of the Association for the Treatment of Sexual Addiction and Compulsivity (ATSAC). ATSAC provides information and offers support on sex addiction and compulsivity.

Richard Gill initially trained and worked at Hazelden in Minnesota USA in 1988/9 with people with various addictions. On returning to the UK he headed the clinical team at the St Joseph's hospital addiction unit in Haselmere, Surrey whilst also carrying out work at the Priory Hospital Roehampton. He then set up and ran for five years the SHARP addiction treatment programme in London which is now part of Action on Addiction. During this period he supervised the Maya Project for women in Peckham whilst training at The Bowlby Centre. As chair of the accreditation committee for the National Association of Drug and Alcohol Counsellors he became involved in the growth of centres for addiction in Europe, South Africa, New Zealand, and the Caribbean. He now works in private practice as an attachment-based psychotherapist in central London.

Lynn Greenwood has fifteen years experience of working with people with complex difficulties, including those labelled as having personality disorders, dissociative disorders, and eating disorders. She is a consultant psychotherapist to the Clinic for Dissociative Studies and a psychotherapist and supervisor in private practice. She has worked in the NHS (South West London & St. George's Mental Health NHS Trust) and private hospitals (The Priory, Huntercombe, Maidenhead), written widely and edited *Violent Adolescents*, (Karnac, 2005). Lynn consults to the television industry and has worked on over ninety series, assessing potential contributors and providing on-going psychological advice, support and management. She is also a performed playwright.

Dr Bob Johnson has been a consultant psychiatrist for twenty-one years, and prior to that a principal in general practice, also for twenty-one years. He has made a special study of the long term impact of trauma, especially with respect to psychopathy and psychosis. He has had extensive medico-legal experience and now runs a small clinic accumulating video and other material for training packs and workshops.

Liz Karter is a leading therapist in gambling addiction, specialising in gambling and how it affects women. Working in the field since 2001 with the leading agencies in the UK and in private practice, Liz established the first women's groups for problem gambling. She has appeared on numerous radio and TV programmes as a specialist in this particular field and is a regular conference speaker and writer. Liz is author of *Women and Problem Gambling: Therapeutic Insights into Understanding Addiction and Treatment*, published in March 2013.

Professor Edward Khantzian is a clinical professor of psychiatry, Harvard Medical School. He is president and chairman of the board of directors of Physician Health Services, a subsidiary of the Massachusetts Medical Society. Dr Khantzian is one of the founders of the American Academy of Addiction Psychiatry, is a past-president of that organisation, and recipient of its Founder Award for his "courage in changing the way we think of and understand addictions." His studies, publications, and teaching have gained him recognition for his contributions on self-medication factors and self-care deficits in substance use disorders and the importance of modified techniques in group therapy for those who abuse substances.

Professor Arlene Vetere is professor of clinical psychology at Surrey University, UK, and professor of family therapy and systemic practice at Diakonhjemmet University College, Oslo, Norway. She is an HCPC (Health and Care Professions Council) registered clinical psychologist, UKCP (UK Council for Psychotherapy) registered systemic psychotherapist and AFT (Association for Family Therapy & Systemic Practice) UK registered systemic supervisor. She is interested in the integration of systems theory and practice with attachment theory and narrative theory and their application across a range of clinical settings. Her recent book with Rudi Dallos, *Systemic Therapy and Attachment Narratives* (Routledge, 2009) is under revision for a second edition. She has worked for over ten years in a community alcohol service and uses her experience with the applications of attachment theory in her approach to problems of substance use.

Kate White is a training therapist, supervisor, teacher, and formerly chair of the Clinical Training Committee at The Bowlby Centre. She is also the editor of the journal, *Attachment: New Directions in Psychotherapy and Relational Psychoanalysis and Series*, and editor of *The John Bowlby Memorial Conference Monographs*.

Prior to training as a psychotherapist Kate was a senior lecturer at The South Bank University, London, in the Department of Nursing and Community Health Studies. She has used her extensive experience in adult education to contribute to the innovative psychotherapy curriculum developed at The Bowlby Centre. In addition to working as an individual psychotherapist, Kate writes about psychotherapy education and runs workshops on the themes of attachment and trauma in clinical practice. Informed by her experience of growing up in South Africa, she has long been interested in the impact of race and culture on theory and on clinical practice. She has edited three books, *Unmasking Race, Culture and Attachment in the Psychoanalytic Space; What do we see? What do we think? What do we feel?* (Karnac, 2006) and *Touch: Attachment and the Body.* (Karnac, 2004), *Talking Bodies: How do we integrate working with the body in psychotherapy from an attachment and relational perspective?* (Karnac, 2013) and co-edited three others, one with Joseph Schwartz, *Sexuality and Attachment in Clinical Practice,* (Karnac, 2007), a second with Sarah Benamer *Trauma and Attachment* (Karnac, 2008) and a third with Judy Yellin, *Shattered States, Disorganised Attachment and its Repair* (Karnac, 2012).

Jason Wright has worked as a psychoanalytic psychotherapist for twenty years, following a pluralistic model. He was CEO and clinical director at the Core Trust addictions charity for twelve years, served on the Drugscope and London Drugs and Alcohol Network boards and held the post of chair of what is now The Council for Psychoanalysis and Jungian Analysis. He currently serves on the board of the College of Psychoanalysis and chairs The Psychoanalytic Consortium. He trained at the Association of Independent Psychotherapists, and has an MA in intercultural and group analytic psychotherapy through Goldsmiths College. He has also sustained a general psychotherapy practice since 1993 founding the group practice "number 42" in London Bridge.

INTRODUCTION

Richard Gill

Another title for the conference might have been "Is addiction a search for a secure base?" A place identified by John Bowlby as fundamental in the healthy development of a person's life since we have attachment needs as he said, "from the cradle to the grave". The question is then "Does addiction provide the soothing and safety which are the features of an internalised secure base and from which the person can then emerge and engage in exploration?" To a person experiencing an addiction the illusory response is yes, it is a necessity. To the onlooker no, its understood in many different ways that result in continuing condemnation, scorn, and controversy which is so easily internalised by the person with an addiction as shame, thus exacerbating it even further. The twentieth John Bowlby Memorial Conference is an attempt to ground the understanding of addiction in a secure enough place so that the aetiology of a person's addiction can be understood as resulting initially from a place of broken attachment relationships.

How these affect the individual in their suffering and isolation is usually hidden and often it is not until they manifest in the form of an out of control behaviour that intervention can take place. Intervention, like the addiction itself, can come in many forms from familial concern to criminal imprisonment with little attention being given to the underlying causes. Similarly there are also many forms which clinical interventions can take, however all can be better understood from understanding how a particular individual's earliest attachment relationships initially developed. The papers that follow are the result of the conference's attempt to understand addiction not only intrapsychically but to locate it within the context of an individual's response to their earliest relationship with their primary attachment figure.

The historical context of addiction was initially explored in the conference by Jason Wright who looked specifically at the use of drugs and alcohol through the ages whilst highlighting the huge growth of a "pain reliever" around the time of the industrial revolution. It is argued in his paper that this industrialisation of society, with the imposition of an established religion and its morality used to control the ever growing work force, produced an aftermath in the present day of judgement and increasing hatred of the self. Thus in Jason's work in the group treatment setting, attachment needs are met through the community of the "like-minded" which allows the individual to work psychodynamically within a psycho-spiritual model. The need for a spiritual dimension in working with those with an addiction is required it is argued because of the many years of attachment to the "dead object" of a mood altering substance, a substance that further crushes a healthy sense of self through shame and condemnation. He has found that the Jungian use of archetype and myth can be reflected and worked with in the group by allowing the "elders of the community" to gain self-worth and self-respect by passing on their experience to those who have recently joined the community and who are in the process of learning to ask for help.

Edward Khantzian's ground-breaking work in understanding addiction has "de-demonised" addiction and the addict. The history of this dates back to the trauma and tragedy of the war in Vietnam. In this period many returning soldiers suffered with post-traumatic stress, often medicated by drugs and alcohol. While treating them the link was made to earlier traumas and broken attachments caused by environmental deprivation in one form or another. The world of addiction was thus turned on its head. Through Khantzian's courageous clinical insight, addiction could be seen as pain relieving not pleasure seeking. This has had huge implications for all but especially the clinician, helping to alter the countertransference so that feelings of condemnation do not contaminate but inform therapeutic interventions. This approach became known as the "Self-Medication Hypothesis" which later identified the use of specific chemicals to regulate specific feeling states. These feeling states were often those that had been difficult to manage in early life as is so often observed in the study of infants of broken attachments. Thus addiction is a signpost to earlier suffering and can be seen as the human being's struggle to survive not as the end result of selfish indulgence.

Arlene Vetere introduced the powerful and careful work of intervening in a person's addiction by way of the family. Great skill has to be employed so as not to alienate either the person with the addiction or the family. This Arlene demonstrated so movingly in her presentation. Working as a systemic psychotherapist she is well aware that alcohol is used within the family as an affect regulation strategy, a means to self soothe and comfort, in response to a deficit in the person's early attachment relationship. They have not learned to trust that others can meet those needs but to trust that alcohol can, no matter how short term the solution may be. So the person with an addiction's primary relationship is with alcohol and her task is to help make them feel safe enough to begin to take emotional risks so as to begin to trust that others in the family can be responsive to them.

Systemic thinking sees the family as a resource and attachment theory guides the therapeutic interventions in seeking the attachment significance of past and current interactions, when people are hurt and disappointed, both in themselves and others. Arlene Vetere showed in her study, how the integration of attachment theory with systemic theory and practice provides a richer explanation of the development and maintenance of alcohol use problems in families, and points to more effective interventions.

Lynn Greenwood's presentation introduced us to her client Debbie and although her main way of seeking control over her life was through food this only covered up a multitude of painful addictions that reflected her isolation and the sense of helplessness within her internal world.

Abandonment, derision, isolation, contempt, and despair were movingly described in Lynn's work with Debbie and she illustrated very clearly the fortitude and suffering people with an addiction necessarily endure as they continue through therapy to make sense of the unknown misuse of power they have encountered in their early life.

The painstaking work by Lynn to hold Debbie after her hospital treatment was emotionally challenging to the end. Debbie's difficulty in letting go of early attachment patterns and subsequent learned coping behaviours left her metaphorically "holding the baby" that had been abandoned so early by her father under the care of an extremely young and insecure mother. Debbie learned as a child to care for her mother and started behaviours that later on harmed her. So challenging was Debbie's fear of becoming attached that Lynn courageously modified her usual practice in order for the emotional bonds to be strengthened whilst together they made sense of her addictions. It was also heartening to see that some of the control that Debbie had learned was channeled into a burgeoning career whilst the repair of her insecure attachment pattern strengthened her relationship with her partner.

Intervention takes place in many settings but nowhere more intense than in a prison. Bob Johnson spent many years as a psychiatrist attending to the mental health needs of a very troubled and often violent group of male prisoners. He saw the fear of facing their addiction as the fear of who they would become if they desisted as it would put them in touch with not only who they had become through their addiction, but the unknown terror that had been for ever present in their lives. He relates several short vignettes of working with identifying early traumatic experiences of these offenders in a specific way that led to the loosening of the grip of their addiction. He likens the treatment approach to that of a disease, the medicine being the release of the terror of early lived trauma and the re-establishment of trust, the trust that has been absent in broken attachments.

The need for establishing trust is apparent in my own chapter describing the work with people of multiple addictions in a daycare setting. The safety here being provided by identification with others and the containing structure of the "twelve step" movement of the Anonymous Fellowships. As identified by Jason Wright there is a need, in my view, for a psycho-spiritual dimension to fill an absence for this group of people recovering from addiction. An absence of wellbeing resulting from early neglect and trauma which then caused the terror that had previously been held at bay by chemicals or self abusive behaviour. However, the denial of the consequences of the addiction needs to be worked with as well and the simple steps of the twelve step programme provided a safe enough container within which the person with an addiction can face the shame and humiliation that has been so repetitious in their lives. The rebuilding of most aspects of their internal and external world is difficult, so continuing support is essential. The

Fellowships provide this on a round the clock basis to support recovery and facilitate guidance to foster the growth of trust in themselves and others.

The internet has provided women with a new means of addiction by way of gambling which Liz Karter explored through her account of her work with a client. The very private access to online gambling sites provides women with a means to continue a cycle of hope and despair that is the basis of all addictions. The isolated use of the internet covers up the shame, guilt, and pain experienced in human relationships so the need for careful building of trust through a women's group provides a powerful antidote.

Technology is again exploding one of the oldest and most difficult of addictions, addiction to sex, especially amongst the young. Cara Crossan describes how quickly this behaviour can take hold and how the many forms of cyber communication provide secrecy.

Although just a few of the human behaviours that can lead to an addiction were explored in the conference it was apparent that they all at their core grew from broken attachments and trauma. It was the hope of all those present that viewing the problem from this perspective would allow society to become more aware that the pain and shame that those with an addiction carry belongs not only to them, but is the result of how society treats the breakdown in early attunement and later emotional communication difficulties on an individual, worldwide and everyday level.

We are delighted to be in a position to bring all these excellent contributions together in this publication so that the fundamental understanding of addiction as a response to early attachment breakdown can be more widely shared so as to alleviate the suffering arising from addictions through the provision of effective attachment informed interventions.

CHAPTER ONE

Attachment theory and The John Bowlby Memorial Lecture 2013: a short history*

Kate White

This year marks twenty years since the first John Bowlby Memorial Lecture was given by Colin Murray-Parkes on the theme of mourning and loss. That was a fitting recognition of Bowlby's great contribution to the understanding of human grief and sadness, while his clinical observations of separation and loss laid down the foundations of attachment theory.

This year's lecturer is Edward Khantzian a pioneer of how addiction has come to be understood as a process of self-medication which has fundamentally changed the way it is treated. He is a clinical professor of psychiatry of Harvard Medical School and one of the founders of the American Academy of Addiction Psychiatry. His view is that people who are addicted are "in need of being understood not so much as pleasure seekers or self-destructive characters, but more as individuals who are in pain and seek and need contact and comfort". (Khantzian, 2014, p. 33 this volume) The roots of addiction, in his view, lie in early attachment and relational trauma.

---

*Based on an original article by Bernice Laschinger.

In the years which have followed the first conference in 1993, attachment theory, in the words of Cassidy and Shaver has produced "one of the broadest, most profound and most creative lines of research in 20th-century (and now 21st-century) psychology" (Cassidy & Shaver, 2008, p. xi). Nevertheless, given the hostility of the psychoanalytic establishment to Bowlby's ideas, it has only been in the last two decades, during which there have been dramatic advances in the congruent disciplines of infancy research and relational psychoanalysis, that the clinical relevance of attachment theory has been unquestionably established.

Indeed, it has been the development of its clinical applications, in tandem with its evolving convergence with psychoanalysis and trauma theory, that has been central to our practice at The Bowlby Centre. Looking back, our very early links with Bowlby's work were forged by one of our founders, John Southgate, who had clinical supervision with John Bowlby. Bowlby's understanding of the nature of human relatedness became primary in our theoretical framework and practice. It contributed directly to our emergence as an attachment-based psychoanalytic centre in 1992.

In 2007 The John Bowlby Memorial Conference marked the centenary of John Bowlby's birth in 1907. One of the outstanding psychoanalysts of the twentieth century, as a theory builder and reformer, his societal impact and influence on social policy have been greater than that of any other. He has been described by Diamond and Blatt (1999, p. 669) as "the Dickens of psychoanalytic theory": he illuminated the human experiences of attachment and loss as vividly as Dickens represented those of poverty and deprivation.

The origins of Bowlby's work lay in his early work with children displaced through war or institutionalisation. This led him to the conviction that at the heart of traumatic experience lay parental loss and prolonged separation from parents. His landmark report for the World Health Organization, *Maternal Care and Mental Health*, enabled him to establish definitively the primary link between environmental trauma and the disturbed development of children (1952).

With these understandings, he entered the public arena to bring about change in the way childhood suffering was addressed by the adult world. Bowlby's work created a bridge over the chasm between individual and social experience and hence between the personal and the political.

There is congruence between the social and therapeutic perspectives of John Bowlby and those of The John Bowlby Memorial Lecturer in 2008, Judith Herman, author of *Father Daughter Incest* (2000) and *Trauma and Recovery* (1992). She, too, has directed her life's work to the "restoring of connections" between the private and public worlds in which traumatic experience takes place; but her focus has been on the traumatic experiences that take place in adulthood. She has shown the parallels between private terrors such as rape and domestic violence and public traumas such as political terrorism. Her conceptual framework for psychotherapy with traumatised people points to the major importance of attachment in the empowerment of the survivor. She writes: "Recovery can take place only within the context of relationships; it cannot occur in isolation" (Herman, 1992, p. 133).

Bowlby had also sought to bridge the chasm between clinician and researcher. His preparedness to leave the closed world of psychoanalysis of his time in order to make links with other disciplines such as animal studies and academic psychology was vital in the building up of attachment theory. The documented and filmed sequence of children's responses to separation in terms of protest, detachment, and despair, as researched by James Robertson, provided evidence of separation anxiety. The impact of these ideas on the development of care of children in hospital has been enormous. The 2001 John Bowlby Memorial Lecturer, Michael Rutter, discussed institutional care and the role of the state in promoting recovery from neglect and abuse. His lecture was a testament to the continuing relevance of Bowlby's thinking to contemporary social issues.

Although Bowlby joined the British Psychoanalytical Society in the 1930s and received his training from Joan Riviere and Melanie Klein, he became increasingly sceptical of their focus on the inner fantasy life of the child rather than real life experience, and tended towards what would now be termed a relational approach. Thus, in searching for a theory which could explain the anger and distress of separated young children, Bowlby turned to disciplines outside psychoanalysis such as ethology. He became convinced of the relevance of animal and particularly primate behaviour to our understanding of the normal process of attachment. These relational concepts presented a serious challenge to the closed world of psychoanalysis in the 1940s, and earned Bowlby the hostility of his erstwhile colleagues for several decades.

The maintenance of physical proximity by a young animal to a preferred adult is found in a number of animal species. This suggested to Bowlby that attachment behaviour has a survival value, the most likely function of which is that of care and protection, particularly from predators. It is activated by conditions such as sickness, fear, and fatigue. Threat of loss leads to anxiety and anger; actual loss to anger and sorrow. When efforts to restore the bond fail, attachment behaviour may diminish, but will persist at an unconscious level and may become reactivated by reminders of the lost adult, or new experiences of loss.

Attachment theory's basic premise is that, from the beginning of life, the baby human has a primary need to establish an emotional bond with a caregiving adult. Attachment is seen as a source of human motivation as fundamental as those of food and sex. Bowlby postulated that "Attachment behaviour is any form of behaviour that results in a person attaining or maintaining proximity to some other preferred and differentiated individual ... While especially evident during early childhood, attachment behaviour is held to characterise human beings from the cradle to the grave" (Bowlby, 1979, p. 129).

Attachment theory highlights the importance of mourning in relation to trauma and loss. An understanding of the relevance of this to therapeutic practice was a vital element in the foundation of The Bowlby Centre. The consequences of disturbed and unresolved mourning processes was a theme taken up by Colin Murray Parkes when he gave the first John Bowlby Memorial Lecture in 1993.

Mary Ainsworth, an American psychologist who became Bowlby's lifelong collaborator, established the interconnectedness between attachment behaviour, caregiving in the adult, and exploration in the child. While the child's need to explore, and the need for proximity might seem contradictory, they are in fact complementary. It is the mother's provision of a secure base, to which the child can return after exploration, which enables the development of self-reliance and autonomy. Ainsworth developed the Strange Situation Test for studying individual differences in the attachment patterns of young children. She was able to correlate these to their mother's availability and responsiveness. Her work provided both attachment theory and psychoanalysis with empirical support for some basic premises. This provided the necessary link between attachment concepts and their application to individual experience in a clinical setting.

Over the last two decades the perspective of attachment theory has been greatly extended by the work of Mary Main who was another John Bowlby Memorial Lecturer. She developed the Adult Attachment Interview in order to study the unconscious processes which underlie the behavioural pattern of attachment identified by Mary Ainsworth. Further support came from the perspective of infant observation and developmental psychology developed by yet another John Bowlby Memorial Lecturer, Daniel Stern. The John Bowlby Memorial Lecturer for 2000, Allan Schore, presented important developments in the new field of neuro-psychoanalysis, describing emerging theories of how attachment experiences in early life shape the developing brain.

The links between attachment theory and psychoanalysis have also been developed. Jo Klein, a great supporter of The Bowlby Centre and also a former contributor to The John Bowlby Memorial Conference, has explored these links in psychotherapeutic practice. In particular, the 1998 Bowlby Lecturer, the late Stephen Mitchell, identified a paradigm shift away from drive theory within psychoanalysis. His proposed "relational matrix" links attachment theory to other relational psychoanalytic theories which find so much resonance in the current social and cultural climate. Within this area of convergence, between attachment research and developmental psychoanalysis, the 1999 John Bowlby Memorial Lecturer, Peter Fonagy, has developed the concept of "mentalisation", extending our understanding of the importance of the reflective function, particularly in adversity.

In similar vein, the work of Beatrice Beebe, the 2001 John Bowlby Memorial Lecturer, represents another highly creative development in the unfolding relational narrative of the researcher-clinician dialogue. Her unique research has demonstrated how the parent–infant interaction creates a distinct system organised by mutual influence and regulation which are reproduced in the adult therapeutic relationship.

In the movement to bring the body into the forefront of relational theory and practice, the 2003 John Bowlby Memorial Lecturer, Susie Orbach, has been a leading pioneer. It was the publication of her groundbreaking books, *Fat is a Feminist Issue* (1978) and *Hunger Strike* (1986) which introduced a powerful and influential approach to the study of the body in its social context. Over the last decade, one of her major interests has been the construction of sexuality and bodily experience in the therapeutic relationship.

The 2004 John Bowlby Memorial Lecturer, Jody Messler Davies, has made major contributions to the development of the relational model. Her integration of trauma theory and relational psychoanalysis led to new understandings of the transference-countertranference as a vehicle for expressing traumatic experience (Davies & Frawley, 1994).

Kimberlyn Leary, our John Bowlby Memorial Lecturer in 2005, illuminated the impact of racism on the clinical process. The importance of her contribution lay in her understanding of the transformative potential inherent in the collision of two "racialised subjectivities" in the therapeutic process. She showed the possibility for reparation when both therapist and client break the silence surrounding their difference.

The contribution of the 2006 John Bowlby Memorial Lecturer, Bessel van der Kolk, to the understanding of post-traumatic stress as a developmental trauma disorder has been seminal, (2005). His book, *Psychological Trauma*, was the first to consider the impact of trauma on the entire person, integrating neurobiological, interpersonal, and social perspectives. (Van der Kolk, 1987).

Within this tradition of great trauma theorists, the contribution of John Bowlby Memorial Lecturer, 2007, Judith Herman, a collaborator of Bessel van der Kolk, has been outstanding. As a teacher, researcher, and clinician, her life's work has been directed to survivors of trauma. Her landmark book, *Trauma and Recovery* (1992) is considered to have changed the way we think about trauma. Bridging the world of war veterans, prisoners of war, and survivors of domestic and sexual abuse, she has shown that psychological trauma can only be understood in a social context.

In 2008 our John Bowlby Memorial Lecturer was Arietta Slade, a widely published clinician, researcher, and teacher. Her work has been enormously significant in the movement to link attachment theory with clinical ideas (1999b, 2008). She has pioneered attachment-based approaches to clinical work with both adults and children, including the development of parental reflective functioning and the relational contexts of play and early symbolisation. There is also a congruence between her current work and the spirit of Bowlby's early clinical observations. She has shifted the therapeutic focus away from the formal categorisation of attachment patterns, to questions about how the attachment system functions to regulate fear and distress within the therapeutic process, significantly where there are "dynamic disruptions".

Arietta Slade's work represents a highly significant development in the application of attachment theory to clinical work (1999a). Following on the work of Main (1994) and Fonagy (1999) she has demonstrated how an attachment-based understanding of the development of representation and affect regulation in the child and his or her mother offers us potentially transformative insights into the nature of the therapeutic process and change.

In 2009 we were honoured to welcome Amanda Jones to give The John Bowlby Memorial Lecture. She presented her work with troubled parents and their children—highlighted in the television series *Help me Love My Baby*. Her work has been acclaimed for its capacity to demonstrate the effectiveness of interventions where the parent is offered a long term compassionate attachment relationship in which their own story of trauma is shared. This provides a possibility for reflectiveness and intergenerational change.

Our John Bowlby Memorial Lecturer in 2010 was Jude Cassidy, a pioneer in the attachment tradition of research with clinical applications. She was a student of Bowlby's primary collaborator Mary Ainsworth and has extended attachment theory's reach in both the fields of childhood and adolescence. As an author and editor she has had a prominent role in the publication of attachment theory, research findings and their clinical application. Jude Cassidy, professor of psychology at the University of Maryland, and director of the Maryland Child and Family Development Laboratory, received her Ph.D. in 1986 from the University of Virginia where her mentor was Mary Ainsworth. Jude Cassidy's research includes a focus on early intervention. Her concerns are wide ranging focusing on attachment, social, and emotional development in children and adolescents, social information-processing, peer relations, and longitudinal prediction of adolescent risk behaviour. These were all areas that were pertinent to our theme in 2009 of Attachment in the Twenty-first Century; Where Next?

In 2011 The John Bowlby Memorial Lecturer was Dr Sandra L. Bloom, who has a long association with The Bowlby Centre as she has been our consultant on trauma for many years. Sandy Bloom is a psychiatrist, currently associate professor of health management and policy and co-director of the Center for Nonviolence and Social Justice at the School of Public Health of Drexel University in Philadelphia. She is best known to us through her imaginative and pioneering work for twenty-one years as director of *The Sanctuary* programmes, an inpatient mental health intervention for adults maltreated as children. Here she developed a humane and compassionate centre caring for those traumatised in early life using the work of John Bowlby as its central conceptual framework. An account of this work is to be found in her publications, Bloom (2013) and Bloom and Farragher (2010, 2013).

Last year Pat Ogden delivered the nineteenth John Bowlby Memorial Lecture on the theme of the links between attachment, trauma, and the body. Her work uses a variety of approaches which focus on the physical as well as the psychological aspects of trauma providing an integration which she has written about with colleagues in their book *Trauma and the Body: A Sensorimotor Approach to Psychotherapy.* (Ogden, Minton & Pain, 2006) Her work is informed by contemporary research in neuroscience, attachment theory, trauma, and related fields.

This year we welcome Edward Khantzian who has, in the years of his exploration into addiction, mapped out so clearly how early trauma leads to addiction. (Khantzian, 1985, 1995 & 1997) In being awarded the Founder Award by the American Academy of Addiction and Psychiatry for his courage in changing the way we think and understand addictions, the link between the work of John Bowlby's attachment theory and addiction has been made.

References

Bloom, S. L. (2013). *Creating Sanctuary: Toward the Evolution of Sane Societies,* 2nd Edition. New York: Routledge.

Bloom, S. L., & Farragher, B. (2010). *Destroying Sanctuary: The Crisis in Human Service Delivery Systems.* New York: Oxford University Press.

Bloom, S. L., & Farragher, B. (2013). *Restoring Sanctuary: A New Operating System for Trauma-Informed Systems of Care.* New York: Oxford University Press.

Bowlby, J. (1952). *Maternal Care and Mental Health,* 2nd Edition. (World Health Organization: Monograph Series, No. 2.) Geneva, Switzerland: World Health Organization.

Bowlby, J. (1979). *The Making and Breaking of Affectional Bonds.* London: Tavistock.

Cassidy, J., & Shaver, P. (2008). *Handbook of Attachment: Theory, Research and Clinical Applications.* New York: Guilford Press.

Davies, J. M., & Frawley, M. G. (1994). *Treating the Adult Survivor of Childhood Sexual Abuse: A Psychoanalytic Perspective.* New York: Basic Books.

Diamond, D., & Blatt, S. J. (1999). Prologue to attachment research and psychoanalysis. *Psychoanalytic Inquiry, 19*(5): 424–447.

Fonagy, P. (1999). Psychoanalytic theory from the point of view of attachment theory and research. In: J. Cassidy & P. R. Shaver (Eds.), *Handbook of Attachment Theory and Research* (pp. 595–624). New York: Guilford Press.

Herman, J. L. (1992). *Trauma and Recovery: The Aftermath of Violence from Domestic Abuse to Political Terror.* New York: Basic Books.

Herman, J. L. (2000). *Father Daughter Incest.* Cambridge, MA: Harvard University Press.

Khantzian, E. J. (1985). The self-medication hypothesis of addictive disorders. *American Journal of Psychiatry, 142*: 1259–1264.

Khantzian, E. J. (1995). Self-regulation vulnerabilities in substance abusers: Treatment implications. In: S. Dowling (Ed.), *The Psychology And Treatment Of Addictive Behavior* (pp. 17–41). New York: International Universities Press.

Khantzian, E. J. (1997). The self-medication hypothesis of substance use disorders: A reconsideration and recent applications. *Harvard Review of Psychiatry, 4*: 231–244.

Main, M. (1994). A move to the level of representation in the study of attachment organization: Implications for psychoanalysis. *Bulletin of the British Psycho-Analytical Society*, 1–15.

Ogden, P., Pain, C., & Minton, K. (2006). *Trauma and the Body: A Sensorimotor Approach to Psychotherapy.* New York: Norton.

Orbach, S. (1978). *Fat is a Feminist Issue.* London: Paddington Press.

Orbach, S. (1986). *Hunger Strike, The Anorectic's Struggle as a Metaphor for Our Time.* London: Faber and Faber.

Slade, A. (1999a). Representation, symbolization and affect regulation. *Psychoanalytic Inquiry, 19*: 797–830.

Slade, A. (1999b). Attachment theory and research. In: J. Cassidy & P. Shaver (Eds.), *Handbook of Attachment: Theory, Research and Clinical Applications* (pp. 575–591). New York: Guilford Press.

Slade, A. (2008). The move from categories to process: Attachment phenomena and clinical evaluation in attachment. *New Directions in Psychotherapy and Relational Psychoanalysis, 2*(1): 89–105.

Van der Kolk, B. (1987). *Psychological Trauma.* Washington, DC: American Psychiatric Press.

Van der Kolk, B. (2005). Developmental trauma disorder. *Psychiatric Annals, 35*(5): 401–408.

CHAPTER TWO

Addiction: treatment and its context

Jason Wright

Given the scope of this essay, the breadth of it's subject and its origins as the opening paper of a conference, I will take a quite personal view of the literature and the field. I start with a quotation which is a reflection of the author Zeyl on the work of Plato's *Timaeus*.

> The well being of the soul in particular is emphasized: it is through realigning the motions of our souls with those of the universe at large that we achieve our goal of living virtuously and happily. (Zeyl, 2013, p. 1)

My contribution will fall into three sections: a description of my work with users, a few vignettes, and a discussion of context. When thinking about how we approach working with someone struggling with addiction, I have found it useful to start from what might be seen as the typical path an addict will follow through their using career.[1] We can use that progression as a structure for thinking, both in terms of appropriate intervention as well as in terms of meaning (much like how one might think about what point an individual is at in their life path when we meet them: youth, middle age or old age, pre or post children, in or out of a relationship). So my approach to the practical work undertaken with addicts, as shown in the vignettes I use as examples, follows this form as does my thinking about the context for our work.

Work with users

My main experience of working with those suffering with addiction comes from running the CORE trust in Marylebone from 1994 to 2006. (CORE is an acronym for Courage to stop, Order in life, Release from addiction and Entry into new life). During my time there we built a multidisciplinary model, working with psychotherapy and complementary therapies in a community setting. CORE's approach to addiction, and its treatment in attachment terms, would be framed as a process of attachment and dependency upon the CORE project and its community members, working through some of the inter and intrapsychic problems of its individual members, and then an appropriate separation from the project in the hope and expectation that individual members will form lasting and secure relationships in their home community. As a means of illustrating work with addicts, I will refer to some of the different ways we thought about this work as I go through this chapter.

During my twelve years at CORE, I encountered and tried to understand many therapeutic models. Being responsible for much of the supervision gave me considerable insight into their differences and similarities. I have taken this experience of diverse therapeutic models on to "Number 42", the project I now run in London Bridge. I like to think of the synthesis of these models in terms of a community— a community of ideas and philosophies as much as the community of people—all of which is focused upon the embodied psyche and the community within which it is embedded. Here I am using the notion of community developed by James Hillman in *Archetypal Psychology* (1981), and in Hillman and Moore, *Blue Fire* (1989) who propose a community of internal archetypal structures as much as an external community of people and ancestors. This is framed in terms of a polytheistic approach to the internal world.[2]

Having had such a diverse experience of practice, I am now not so sure of my theoretical allegiances. However, I started as a Jungian and at heart probably remain so. I was originally inspired by Hillman's archetypal work, which fits with a transpersonal meta-perspective for the psyche and its place in our collective being. I still adhere to his idea in *Suicide and the Soul* (Hillman, 1968) that it is the analyst's personal investment in the process that is key. Transpersonal in this sense refers to the psycho-spiritual rather than the group analytic notion of transpersonal.[3] Thoughts of a psycho-spiritual approach to therapy are relevant in that so much of the rhetoric for addiction treatment is set in this context, for instance, the Twelve Step (developed by Alcoholics Anonymous) notion of giving up to your higher power. Importantly, such an idea could usefully be seen as a more personal challenging of the omnipotent features of a psyche at use. Here I mean a psyche using, implying a differentiation between but inclusion of the material and spiritual. This would be the kind of position the twelve steps would adopt. Seeing addiction as a transpersonal issue. This context would take the view that psyche being the greek word for soul is of fundamental importance. I was told again only recently that "It (step one of Alcoholics Anonymous) helpfully let me know that I was not God".

I do not propose to elaborate upon an attachment model at length, I will leave the rest of the conference to take that forward. An attachment model is a vital component of the thinking at CORE with its focus upon attachment, dependence, separation, and loss. I will, however, link my ideas in this essay to Khantzian's (2008) self-medication model, Schore's work on affect regulation (2010), as well as Flores' work (1997, 2004), to ideas that trauma is the root of addiction.

Schore's current book *The Art and Science of Psychotherapy* (2012) is a tour de force, working through a wide range of theory to link current neuroscience research with psychodynamic thinking and our practice as psychotherapists. When considered in conjunction with McGilchrist's (2009) work *The Master and His Emissary* and his differentiation between left and right brain thinking (following on from the work of the seventies but setting it in our current understanding of neuroscience), they offer a perspective that establishes the right brain's all encompassing meta-view. This shows a capacity to hold and contain our interconnected, inter-subjective, interrelatedness, which provides a clear foundation, if one were needed, for psychoanalytic thought in the context of brain science. For me, this has impact not only on the specific individual work in the room, but for our relations as groups and societies.

Five stages of a using career

As I have indicated earlier it is useful to think of treatment in terms of a using career. For convenience, I have separated this into five stages. I do not see this as a determined structure rather, from experience, what seems to happen when working with addicts.

The stages for addiction, as I frame them, are:

1. Using
2. Trying to stop
3. First attempts
4. Stopping, and
5. Working through the underlying causes of the using.

Different tools are best employed at each of these stages. For instance, harm minimisation, cognitive, and educative interventions are best through early stages one, two, three, and the beginnings of stage four, whereas working through the underlying dynamics of using would be for stages three, four, and five. However I would see that all tools point to forming a relationship with the addicted person and framing that relationship beyond their identity as an addict.

It is worth considering here a tension between harm minimisation and abstinence-based models. Harm minimisation agendas are pointed toward reducing the harm drug and alcohol use does to the individual and the community around them, their local community and network of relationships and the wider abstract community. Abstinence-based agendas propose that you have to stop using in order to let go of your addiction. My personal approach is abstinence-based, although not particularly twelve step orientated. My interest is not particularly to reduce harm per se, but to try to get to understand why someone uses. However, my experience shows me that the seduction of cross addiction (swapping one addiction for another e.g., alcohol for cannabis or food for drugs) is too great to get to the underlying dynamics of the addiction. Thus the client needs to be "clean" and remain clean for an extended period to truly work with any underlying dynamics. They need the capacity to contain their personal unconscious experiences before the work of understanding them can begin. This does not mean that the analyst/therapist would not be considering or drawing attention to such dynamics during a period of pre-abstinence.

Currently we live in a world, particularly in the funded sector, that focuses upon harm minimisation and has moved away from abstinence-based approaches. The focus on treatment is different to what it has been historically, the field is less focused upon addressing the underlying dynamics of addiction. I don't intend to rehearse the arguments here or go into the turf and policy wars that have become entrenched over the influx of government money since 1997. David Nutt (2011), in *Drugs Without the Hot Air*, presents an interesting case for the harm minimisation field but appears to dismiss out of hand the psychodynamic model, which Flores (2004), Khantzian (1999), Khantzian and Albenase (2008), Winship (2012), and others elaborate with such eloquence.

Over the last ten or twelve years, the state, in the guise of the National Treatment Agency (NTA) has had considerable impact on treatment, working towards manualisation (the creation of treatments that are presentable in manual form so that they can be disseminated that way) and assisting the process of scaling up interventions to meet a mass market. This has been developed in the funding frames of a business culture and a medical model—I would say a commodified model. Recently, recovery, which was developed as a verb by the twelve step movement, has been co-opted by the state with NTA and David Best's "Routes to Recovery" (2013). This policy shift, both in attitude and delivery, to treatment was precipitated by a change of government but has not really sustained the previous diverse work in the field.

The intervention of the state in this way, working toward manualisation and a one size fits all approach, which can be common to scaling up, presents a problem for the localism of experience and runs the risk of missing out the particular or personal relationship found in psychodynamic thinking. One might argue that this is born out of a focus upon the objective to the detriment of subjective and inter-subjective thinking and the corporate and managerial approach to social problems. Full discussion of this aspect of addiction treatment I think is fundamental to the context of addiction, but beyond the scope of this chapter. I will return to this comodificatory theme, however, later. It might be argued that mass addiction is a response to the constraints of such objectification.

I used to say at CORE that it was "… easy to stop being a drug addict, to stop taking drugs. However, you then may have some human problems which you might want to deal with." This was slightly disingenuous but helped in the differentiation between the human suffering at the root of the using and the struggles with the substance, or for that matter the behaviour of a process addiction.[4]

This process of letting go of addiction, as I have experienced working with it, is orientated toward forming a relationship, fostering a real and alive attachment connection to a living person. The attachment, certainly in the first instance during stages two and three, is likely to be institutional, whether that is to the state through the police, legal system, or social services, or to a voluntary organisation, twelve step, or community-based project. This will then develop on to individual and perhaps more specific group and individual relationships where the internal difficulties can be examined and worked through. One might describe this as various means of containing insecure attachment patterns. The attachment pattern is likely to be formed through difficult early life experiences or traumas. Khantzian and his colleagues make a good case for later traumas triggering a descent into use and elaborate this with regard particularly to Post-Traumatic Stress Disorder. Hopefully, through relationships and time, more secure attachments can be earned. These relationships may initially be forged in the context of the institution where it may be possible to find a consistently available attachment figure that can be depended upon, then mediated through the containment and routine of that institution. An assumption I make here is that of viewing addiction as an attachment to a dependable, but dead object (Rey, 1994; Winship, 2012).

Using will make predictable what you are going to feel and when you are going to feel it. However, in order to have this dependability, you have to sacrifice your life, sometimes literally. The drug, the alcohol, or the behaviour comes first, everything else second. This has considerable impact upon how one might approach the work with addicts. We are human, and however rigid we might be in maintaining our frame, cannot supply the same material and inflexible dependability as the "substance" or process of addiction.

The first four stages, up to the end of rehab, usually require quite focused and probably directive interventions whether that is as simple as telling people not to go down the pub or into the off licence, exploring what triggers using and avoiding these circumstances, altering their friendship networks or working with them to understand how they habitually repeat patterns of behaviour. In my experience, individual relationships developed over this time, whether with other group members or staff, project workers or social workers, are key to establishing the right framework of affect regulation to enable better self-regulation. These interpersonal relationships deepen and begin the foundations of recovery. They begin the process of being able to differentiate and define complex intrapsychic feeling structures whilst providing a framework for containing harmful behaviour. Most importantly, the capacity to begin to bear internal experience can be developed.

There comes a point when a client decides to stop. This is the most productive time in treatment. If one were to follow a twelve step model one might enter rehab. CORE offered treatment for a transient day community, but did not adhere to a twelve step model only. Many who were able to work within the communal setting at CORE found this of use and dealt more easily with the problems of transition back into their home environment. A degree of motivation is necessary to activate a conscious attempt to stay clean and to get to meetings for instance. The important point here is that it is the group, the community, that contains the individual psyche, whether it's the community of CORE or the fellowship of the twelve step movement. The group will hold the individual as they begin to be able to form relationships.

Then there are ten or more long years of working through the underlying psychodynamics, and on into the rest of your life. This can be done in many frames: communal, social, or psychological. One could go to Scotland to plant trees, become involved with the twelve step movement or smart recovery,[5] or enter an analysis. This is the time that psychotherapeutic interventions have their greatest effect on the development of dependable interpersonal relationships which sustain life, its repair, growth, and development.

Seen from a broadly attachment point of view, there is a path of originating trauma, probably but not always early life experiences, leading to a disturbed attachment state of mind. Through attachment and dependence, relationship and a learned capacity to regulate affect, it is possible to separate and develop autonomous dependence on self and relate to others freely, seeking support when needed. This is an idealistic expression of what is a difficult and tortuous journey for all involved. My experience is that a group is needed to achieve this and as therapists we need to find our place in that group to be of real use. There is a way of thinking about addiction that is founded upon a sense of belonging, how we belong and what we belong to, how we fit in in the community of being, whether that is local and personal or more widely drawn socially and culturally. We as therapists need to provide a certain kind of language and a serviceable enough object with which the process of developing a secure enough attachment relationship can take place. However, it is difficult to provide this as an individual as it usually takes a group to contain using. A model of specific personal trauma is useful for working with individuals, but with addiction I would argue that we are caught in a collective group struggle.

CORE provided a community that was capable of holding and thinking about thirty or so people at varying stages of the process of becoming addiction free. All had agreed to be abstinent and all had committed to attending the programme daily in order to become a member of the community. The work of the staff team was to provide a containing frame for the experiences that came up around letting go of use and that needed to be thought about. This process was greatly aided by those clients who had been in the programme for a while and were better able to manage their own experience. They would be able to support those that were newly drug free, providing dependable relationships that were mediated by the community. This cut both ways offering those that were new to the thought that change was possible and those that were further down the line, the realisation that they had the capacity to contain not only their own experience, but the experience of others.

My understanding is that this is also true for the twelve step movement. The core experience that it offers is the communal container of sympathetic and experienced others who, working together, can offer real containment.

So I will offer two vignettes here to show the different stages of letting go of addiction and different aspects of what I have discussed.

Two vignettes

Mr D

History

He tells me that his father could have had an Asperger's diagnosis and that his mother was depressed. He had two brothers younger than him. He was taken to the USA in his early teens where he felt alienated and an outsider. Upon return to the UK he took up cannabis use and gained the identity and role of the one who could get cannabis in his school.

Stage one (using)

Mr D was bright and able to both use and get into university where he developed his habits and range of drug use. After two intense spiritual experiences, he developed and consolidated his habit into heroin use (Wright, 2005).

Stage two (thinking of stopping)

He tried at various times to stop by himself and at one point entered what seemed to be a Kleinian analysis.

Stage three (first attempts)

He had a period of ambivalent attempts to stop at CORE with several relapses. He was able to remain in contact with the project and foster a connection. Some years later he stated that he "Took it as far as I thought I could get away with".

Stage four (stopping)

He formed an attachment to the project and found himself able to use me, stopped using and felt accepted into the community. He worked through the programme developing relationships within the community and the staff team. Toward the end he had a crisis in his personal relationship and resolved this. He left the community with a particularly interesting epiphanal experience that mimicked his entry into truly serious destructive use, but traveling in the reverse direction (Wright, 2005).

This process took eighteen months. He left on a manic high that burnt out after six months.

Stage five (on into the rest of life/ exploration of the underlying psychodynamics)

He came to my private practice. He started work, took on responsibility, expanded his family and developed relationships at work and socially.

He was particularly interested in a transpersonal and psychospiritual context to the work from a psychodynamic perspective. We worked for another few years. He migrated to the couch and deepened his thinking. I moved. He experienced this with some difficulty and it might be said that the initially cold new place by the window ruptured his mind (or repeated the originating rupture).

He developed a clear sense of self that could be considered and worked with.

The work deepened and grew. He is successfully bringing up kids and sustaining a difficult job (business planning in a complex organisation). Work becomes ever more complex and he has to deal with his team and many other workers.

This week we are discussing, after the break, how he has come to have a mind of his own, how he can think and operate in the group not free from but attending to his anxieties and internal dynamics as they present in the team he works in, to work with the team's anxieties. Also, how to differentiate between himself and the context within which he is embedded.

Mr B

History

Mr B's family of origin is small, only him, his mother and his father. His mother had a narcissistic wounding out of which she imposed her mind on Mr B in such a way that for her he was an object of her mind, rather than being a self in his own right. His father was emotionally absent but present in the home until Mr B was aged four at which juncture his father left.

Stage one

He first started using cannabis in his early adolescence at school, over time this eventually developed into a serious cocaine habit. He came to see me when he wanted to stop, making his first serious attempts.

Stage two

He was able to engage and to detox from cocaine without the need for rehab, which he did not want to attend. He continued with his therapy and his work.

Stage three

He continued with his therapy, built a life free from cocaine but continued cannabis use, established a career in the third sector, moved from his houseboat to a flat.

Stage four

He finally gave up cannabis after six years of intermittent and reducing use. During this time he was able to work through the struggles he had had with his parents, develop his career, and built relationships both professional and personal.

Stage five

He took on more powerful jobs, developing his career internationally and widening his network both professionally and with friends and acquaintances. He has taken the work that he has done on himself into his career, developing a consultancy practice and is able to think both dynamically and entrepreneurially.

Historical context

I have already gone too far into the image I am proposing for imagining addiction without setting this in context. I intend to shift the frame here slightly and follow a more collective social and historical thread in order to set the attachment model in context. This research is again personal. Early in my thinking I was interested in the work of Luigi Zoja (1989) who looked etymologically at the word "addict" and saw it rooted in the relationship between the slave and his master in Latin. He developed an argument that we are enslaved, given over to the drug or process of use. He goes on to focus upon addiction, in our current capitalist cultural frame, in terms of consumerist avoidance of the internal life. Damien Thompson has written a journalistic polemic, *The Fix* (2012), which looks at this social phenomenon. They both follow a thread of interrelationships between commodification and alienation which can be seen to begin with the art historian Baumgarten's (1750) aesthetic philosophy, based on his reaction against the commodification of art and its development as a commercial enterprise in the eighteenth century, which has led to the troubles with capitalist commodification and hollowing out of sustaining significant symbols in the current day.

Zoja (1989) developed a Jungian archetypal model for addiction, something which we used at CORE to provide an imaginal frame and context for an individual's use, setting the possibility of a collective frame for both trauma and its containment. In this theoretical train,

Hillman (1983) comments that "you don't heal the person you heal the story". We found this a useful way of framing the journey through addiction. It allowed us to develop a context for collectively experienced trauma expressed through each addicted person. For instance, in Europe, working through the collective trauma of two great wars colours much of our daily life. Some also argue that we struggle with the trauma of the Industrial Revolution and its social changes. Industrialisation and commodification of life can be seen at play in our attitudes to use and using behaviours. David Nutt (2011) approaches this relationship in his book *Drugs Without the Hot Air* making the point that we are currently struggling with industrial strength drugs, that is, opium as heroin, coca as crack etc. However I think he misses the psychodynamic out of his argument, the personal, subjective and related, as his focus is on policy and science, risking, in my opinion a reenactment of addictive dynamics in his thinking. As I write he has aggravated the media (*Telegraph*, 16 April 2013) with comments that the crash of 2007 was cocaine fueled. Whether or not he was misquoted it is difficult to say but it shows the inverted nature of his argument. No doubt there is a great deal of cocaine use in the city, but I doubt that it was the cocaine that fueled the crash, rather the addictive structure and mindset at the root of the greed that fueled the disastrous banking process.

I would be more interested in how the struggle with the social and psychological changes needed to live in an industrial, and now post-industrial culture can be expressed in terms of collective trauma and suggest framing mass addiction as a response to this trauma. The emptying out of symbol into hollow commodity, and the resulting attachment to commodity rather than relationships between individuals or communities is the emptying out of life: Bauldriard's (1994) simulacrum. This can be seen in the riots of eighteen months ago where the rioters took products, Raybans and trainers, not streets and neighbourhoods. Another example might be the turning of life's difficult experiences into medical and insurable commodities of the DSM 5 (Diagnostic and Statistical Manual 5).

The argument that addiction, as we now know it, is a product of industrialisation has some interest. I will return to it. However, if we are to follow addiction etymologically, we first find the word addict as an adjective used in 1520. It then meant "delivered or devoted", delivered over by judicial sentence. By 1600 it meant "tendency, inclination or penchant". It came into its current use with either opium or morphine in 1905/6 except for an isolated incident in 1779 with reference to tobacco. I think the function of addiction in the human psyche goes a long way back into history. Our current approach is a function of where we are in history, socially, culturally, and politically, and not a function of addiction, so it is inevitable we will see it in a post-industrial context.

Some Jungians, Meade (1993) for example, would put forward the idea that the things that we become addicted to were at some point sacred. Alcohol, opium, tobacco, chocolate, etc. Some arguments in this context see addiction as an emptying out of ritual and sacred space emphasising the failure of community to recognise changes in progress through the stations of life. This leaves the individual to routinely participating in a ritual encounter with death as symbol of transformation. Using then becomes a dead ritual for initiation from one life stage to another, for instance girl to woman or boy to man, condemning the addict to repeat this encounter with death with each use in the hope of returning as a transformed being to a community that will see them in their new form. However the community is not there.

This is one transpersonal model for addiction and was useful in the community of CORE, offering us, in a communal context, a frame to recognise individual change that was needed for the move to new life. I understand that Michael Meade (2013) has had some success with this model in gang communities in Chicago and Los Angeles. It would be easy to see how the twelve step movement could offer a similar opportunity.

I now want to go back a little further to make a connection to Plato and the Timaeus dialogues (1997, 2013). In it Socrates notes that there is "one who is absent". Timaeus says he is "sick", and equates the sickness with absence. The dialogue explores Platonic cosmology and a way of imagining the construction of the universe which is not relevant here. However, as the dialogue develops, we begin to infer that the absent party is absent as a result of alcohol, he is drunk and perhaps compulsively so, and this is referred to as the sickness. The link between sickness and absence is interesting. For me it says a lot about how addiction, as we now understand it, is experienced. There is a lack, an absence, what some might see as a void, and this is the sickness, an image for addiction that supports the idea that it is a relational or attachment problem. The narrative might run like this: "something happens in my life to make me believe that I am empty, wrong or bad. I am unfillable and cannot find the resources internally or through others to fill this emptiness. However, I have found this substance, cigarettes, cannabis, alcohol, drugs, sex, work, coffee, cupcakes, etc. which I can imagine for a moment will fill this emptiness for me, replace the broken or unformed part and offer me freedom from that which terrifies me, the relating other." So much in addiction points to the fear of intimacy. Sex Addicts Anonymous (SAA) has a slogan "We fear intimacy greater than death" which is often repeated to me in the session.

Mr B's founding injury was his mother's narcissistic need of him to alleviate her depression and his father leaving the family home when Mr B was four. Mr D's mother's depression after both his and his brother's birth impacted upon him, leading to a similar narcissistic wounding. So there is a compulsion to fill this void with a substance or process. To salve our suffering with something from the outside that will fill us even if only temporarily.

I have looked at this in terms of the concept of attachment to a dead object. Winship has followed a similar path (2012, Kindle location 1365; Rey, 1994). The internal structure of the psyche being formed by early relations with actual objects or people in the world that felt dead. The horror of the original relationship with what Winnicott (1960) might call the facilitating environment was too difficult to bear. This might be understood as a trauma. With Mr D, a depressed and emotionally absent mother and a literally absent father led him to turn to cannabis later in his life. He described an image of lying with his mother as he heard his brother scream in the cot next to them. This was brought up by a change of consulting room and a cold draft from the window referred to earlier. He has described this as the moment he was able to let his mind collapse, to let go of a false "pastiche" mind that had been thrown together with brightness and begin to build a mind of his own. I moved him closer to the radiator. Kalsched's (1996, 2013) ideas of an archetypal spiritual self defence are useful here to understand this process, rooted as it is in Winnicottian (1960, 1964) ideas of true and false self. Kalsched (1996) proposed in *The Inner World of Trauma* an internal archetypal structure that defends the inner core of being, something that a Winnicottian might frame as the true self, from the outside world and any possibility of the repetition of the trauma. Unfortunately, this structure not only isolates the person, it separates them from their core being but it is likely to re-traumatise that being itself. He uses the Rapunzel story as an illustration of how to work with this. The need to bear the attacks of the client are emphasised.

Mr B's mother's need of him as an object of her own psyche, and the father's lack of emotion and then leaving of the home, led to his using and his search for "relationship" in the wrong place. His attachments in school were to the children older than him who would bring cannabis back from Amsterdam. It made him feel included when he sold on their drugs. Unfortunately for the school he was very entrepreneurial, something he has currently turned to good use. For me, Mr B's search for recognition from the group points to the need for the context of community. As I have said earlier, the client will need a group of some kind, be that in twelve step, smart recovery, or a fully committed and supportive family and work environment. I also think the user will need to stop and stop from everything. The seduction of cross addiction, substituting one addiction for another, is too great and usually the terror of true relatedness so demanding that only the focus upon abstinence can meet the discipline required to let go of using. I have had one or two exceptions as patients, a man who was self medicating for ADHD with cocaine comes to mind, but they have been few and far between. This is where the group is so valuable in holding onto consciousness of "using behaviour" and supporting the individual with their struggle not to fall back into compulsive behaviour in whatever form it may present itself.

A substance or process will give you a certain type of experience, both repeatable and importantly, knowable. You will know what you are going to feel and when you are going to feel it. Users will often report that this is exactly the attraction of using. It won't relate back or offer any relational demands. This dynamic offers control and the capacity for denial and avoidance that no human relationship, except perhaps codependence can, but exacerbates the sense of emptiness and internal void, whether narcissistic or existential. I would say, the internal struggle remains unconscious and demonstrated though actions in the external world. Khantzian (2008), Winship (2012) and Flores (1997, 2004) all point to Kohut's (1971) self psychology as a way of framing these particular experiences.

The twelve step movement provides a strong containing frame for work with addiction, but can be vulnerable to being seen as cultish with its insistence upon rigid boundaries and adherence to structure and dogma. Damien Thompson (2011) is virulently anti-twelve step seeing it in this light and presents many of the arguments put forward against the fellowship. He prefers to focus upon cognitive and neuroscientific and "evidence based" explanations for addiction. Nutt (2012) falls into the same trap, likening the effect of a tab of acid to years in the twelve step movement. My reading of addictions runs contrary to this and sees these interpretations missing the relational roots of using. It might be argued that a view of using that denies its relational components could be framed in terms of the very resistance and the enactment of the terror and confusion of forming true relatedness that I am arguing are at root in addiction.

The twelve step movement has developed a governance strategy in the twelve traditions which helps it resist the process of descent into a cult and thereby creates a robust and containing community within which to let go of using, bringing attention to the relational and communal factors that could be seen to be causal in that using. However the fellowship is inhabited by humans and addicted ones at that and is therefore prone to all the madness and confusions that we as humans suffer. The intensely democratic underpinnings of the twelve step structure ensures its diversity, but also the difficulties that that engenders.

Some might suggest that there is a whole counterculture and community around using, a whole economy, perhaps a legitimate economy and social order if we look at drinking. From a social and political viewpoint this is an interesting narrative, but here it is important to look relationally at the using. The "culture" and the relationships in using are dead and a pastiche. Power dynamics are acted out in dealing, they are not relational, the drug is all and the dynamic is essentially sadomasochistic and auto-erotic. In a pub for instance, it all looks very convivial, but no one is relating at all, or at least it is only a few of the regulars. Everyone is relating to the alcohol behind the bar. Here I sometimes get challenged not to throw the baby out with the bath water and that alcohol, for instance, particularly in low doses, dilutes the anxiety of relating and enables communication. This is a difficult call. Too easily this can be the start of a slippery slope. When working one has to judge where a client is with their use. Measurement of units and a drink diary are useful.

Now I will briefly return to the narrative that develops from the Industrial Revolution. The first real explosion of "using" is the gin craze in the first half of the eighteenth century. This was brought about through a period of increased wealth, reduced grain prices and a relaxation of the distilling laws in London. There were a series of Acts of Parliament concluding in 1751 that licensed gin production and sale. Some think that it was the increase in food prices that stopped the high levels of consumption. This is depicted in Hogarth's engravings Gin Lane and Beer Street (1751) which are seen in terms of the afflictions of the poor.

Following this forward, Rowdy Yates (2012) has developed an argument that follows addiction and its development after the Industrial Revolution. Again, this is seen as a moral collapse of the working classes, followed by the development of the temperance movement and temperance groups seeing addiction as a spiritual and moral problem from the 1830s onward. As we follow this thread it leads us to current characterological, disease, biological, psychological, social, and behavioural models which begin to steer away from moral and class-based assumptions to models of suffering.

Some current thinking in the United States documented in *The House I Live In*, Jarecki (2012), has focused upon the war on drugs as a war upon the disenfranchised and that its outcomes have generated a means of mass incarceration of what we used to call in our wonderful eighties Marxist education "the reserve army of labour". This burgeoning underclass has been formed as corporate America shifted its industrial base to cheaper Eastern manufacturers leaving the traumatised, first black (using Crack), then white (using Crystal Meth), poor to enter the illegitimate economy of drugs to survive. So class narratives are not entirely gone.

Conclusion

We are focusing today on the characterological models which would frame addiction in terms of trauma and personality, and as Khantzian (2008) does, sees addiction as a self medicalising response to internal suffering. I would agree with this wholeheartedly and would add that what I see is that a user won't stop using until the pain of use is as great as the internal suffering and that, try as we might to get in the way, we make precious little difference until that point. Early intervention then would be the most effective way to help someone come to that understanding as soon as possible. Here, cognitive and educative models such as motivational interviewing have most impact. However, I would counsel that this be undertaken with an eye to the underlying psychodynamics as they present themselves.

I am trying to develop the thought that the personal trauma, be that in infant and primary caregiver relationships, or later traumatic experiences, are set in a social and group context, something that can be seen as a more cultural, social, and group trauma. The changes in the social environment that have brought about the way we live currently come at a price that is linked to, and expressed by, the way we relate individually and in groups. Addiction is one of these prices.

Our current economic culture is predicated upon perpetual growth and consumption. From this viewpoint one might argue that the filling of a void left by the changing of our social structures and the dispersal of interconnected social ties makes a breach in the personal and perhaps transpersonal that makes the individual so inflammatory and the family thermonuclear. Zoja (1989) seems to be approaching this position. This atomisation is accelerated with the advent of mass and immediate communication. The other material changes that come with this change in social organisation are of great benefit in terms of longer life and physical security. However we struggle with something that is missing, I would say the connection to others in a manageable, related, human form. We are having to engineer new means of generating our old ties, we need now to find a means of forming communities that can provide the containment to sustain and generate relatedness. I would argue that the whole psychological and psychotherapeutic project is one such technology. Our mass commodified culture strains to come to terms with what is enough in a crowded world. It delivers us products but alienates and divides. It fosters an ideology that an external object or event will solve internal difficulty, will salve inner conflict. This to my mind mirrors what an addict does in their immediate life and drug use. They need to relinquish the using in order to face and come to terms with the underling dynamics and suffering. We would appear to need to let go of perpetual commodity use and growth, perhaps to return to a focus upon relatedness, although in a more conscious and volitional form. In its most obvious context this is a question of numbers. Seven billion humans inhabit our world and this number is growing, there are finite resources in the small bubble that we live in and we are using them up.

Elias (1939, 1978), the sociologist so loved by group analysts, put forward a sociological communitarian theory that proposed the continued civilising development of mankind. Following his theories through, we come to an understanding as to how, within the group, we find our way to creating new and I would say more, democratic means of tackling our cultural and social changes. De Mare, Piper and Thompson (1991) provided, also from a group analytic perspective, a means of understanding the process of this on a large group scale, offering a framework for structure and dialogue. Dialogue, De Mare argues, is the fundamental process by which the transformation of psychic energy takes place in the large group. The process of change can be schematised as "Frustration—hate—psychic energy—dialogue—thinking—understanding—information—Koinonia." The model for this process is reminiscent of a Freudian model for the psyche. Bioculture, socioculture, ideoculture are group structures, it is argued, that are correspondent to the id (collective archetypal level in Jungian theory), superego and ego of the personal psyche or mind. The bioculture of the group represents the archetypal level of the group unconscious. The socioculture manifests the wider cultural attitudes and functions much as the superego would in the personal unconscious. The ideoculture formed by the group over time through the conflicted interaction of the bioculture and the socioculture, acts as the ego and holds and sustains the koinonic atmosphere. The twelve step movement is a highly democratic example of this process at work. At CORE the embodied minds of the members of the community come together to form an environment where the difficult and uncontainable affect of some of its members can be considered. At "Number 42" we try to continue this work in a different context. I would frame this with a model that is more archetypally based than Freudian, following the work of Hillman and looking for unifying archetypal images upon which to found dialogue in large group formations.

From my personal experience, it seems to take a sacrifice of personal identity to help hold this process, to find a way of differentiating what one imagines to be one's own need and what the group needs from you. From what I have seen with addiction too, something of this sacrifice has to be made. One has to give up a clinging to identity to be more whole and more whole in relation to the group. Isolation is no longer a possibility or return to use is inevitable.

Following the logic of this chapter, describing how culturally and personally we come to be at this place with addiction, and looking from a teleological point of view, the struggle with addiction might offer us, as a group and individuals, a window on the struggle with the culture we have built and the suffering and traumas that that engenders for us en masse. The things addicts have to let go of and come to terms with in terms of human suffering go some way to offering a paradigm for examining current cultural and social change as we form new ways to bear our suffering and relate.

Notes

1. It is common in addiction treatment circles to refer to the journey through using as a "career".
2. Many Jungians have traditionally been interested in the Greek pantheon, and often discuss these ideas in the context of Western thought. This Eurocentrism points to the local nature of psychoanalysis, in a European context. I would argue Asian, African, or Pre-Colombian narratives are equally useful, but are embedded in their own cultural context. Where they meet of course, a narrative develops between the two. What of this is truly archetypal and common to all is an interesting question: for instance we all had mothers (even if separated at birth) and we all form communities.
3. Transpersonal in a psycho-spiritual perspective is a psychotherapeutic tradition orientated toward the incorporation of religious or spiritual experiences "Transpersonal theory is concerned with the study of transpersonal and spiritual dimensions to human nature and existence" (Ferra, 2002, p. 5) ... "... a Fourth psychology, transpersonal, trans human, centred in the cosmos rather than in human needs and interests, going beyond humanness, identity, self-actualisation, and the like" (Maslow, 1968, pp. iii–iv). Jungian theory could be considered transpersonal and Alan Mulhearn (2012) gives an interesting account of the spiritual in healing from a broadly Jungian perspective. The group analytic notion of transpersonal is oriented to the group and above the personal. There is more to be explored between the overlap of each term. The contrast between the Jungian collective unconscious and Hopper's (2003) social unconscious might evidence this difference.
4. Process addictions are those that are not related to chemicals such as drugs or alcohol. So they might be gambling, shopping, or sex addiction for instance.
5. SMART Recovery (Self Management and Recovery Training) is an international non-profit organisation which provides assistance to individuals seeking abstinence from addictive behaviours. The approach used is secular and science-based using non-confrontational motivational, behavioural, and cognitive methods.

References

Bauldriard, J. (1994). *Simulacra and Simulation*, Ann Arbor: The University of Michigan Press.

Baumgarten, G. A. (1750). *Aesthetica*, volume 2. (1750–1758). Stanford encyclopedia of philosophy. http://plato.stanford.edu/entries/aesthetics-18th-german/#Bau (Last accessed 4 December 2013).

Best, D. (2013). Routes to recovery. NTA. http://www.nta.nhs.uk/routes-to-recovery.aspx. Last accessed in 2013. (NTA is now part of Public Health England).

Dalal, F. (2001). The social unconscious: A post-Foulkesian perspective. *Group Analysis, 34*: 539–555.

De Mare, P., Piper, R., & Thompson, S. (1991). *Koinonia: From Hate, Through Dialogue, to Culture in the Large Group*. London: Karnac.

Elias, N. (1939, 1978). *The Civilising Process, Volume 1, The History of Manners*. New York: Urizen.

Elias, N. (1939, 1982). *The Civilising Process, Volume 2, Power and Civility*. New York: Pantheon.

Ferra, J. (2002). *Revisioning Transpersonal Theory: A Participatory Vision of Human Spirituality*. Albany, NY: SUNY.

Flores, P. (1997). *Group Psychotherapy with Addicted Populations*. New York: Haworth Press.

Flores, P. (2004). *Addiction as an Attachment Disorder*. New York: Aronson.

Gerhardt, S. (2004). *Why Love Matters*. Hove: Routledge.

Gin Craze of the 18th century, Alcohol: First report of session 2009–10, House of Commons Health Committee, 10 December, 2009. www.publications.parliament.uk/pa/cm200910/cmselect/cmhealth/151/15111. html a32 Last accessed in 2013.

Hillman, J. (1968). *Suicide and the Soul*. London: Hodder & Stoughton.

Hillman, J. (1975). *Revisioning Psychology*. London: Harper Row.

Hillman, J. (1981). *Archetypal Psychology: A Brief Account*. Dallas: Spring Publications.

Hillman, J. (1983). *Healing Fiction*. New York: Stanton Hill Press.

Hillman, J., & Moore, T. (1989). *A Blue Fire: The Essential James Hillman*. London: Routledge.

Hopper, E. (2001). The social unconscious: Theoretical considerations. *Group Analysis, 34*(1): 9–27.

Hopper, E. (2003). *The Social Unconscious: Selected Papers*. London: Jessica Kingsley.

Kalsched, D. (1996). *The Inner World of Trauma: Archetypal Defense of the Personal Spirit*. London: Routledge.

Khantzian, E., & Albanese, M. (2008). *Understanding Addiction as Self Medication*. New York: Rownam & Littlefield.

Kohut, H. (1971). *The Analysis of the Self*. New York: International University Press.

Maslow, A. (1968). *Towards a Psychology of Being*. New York: Van Nostrand.

McGilchrist, I. (2009). *The Master and His Emissary: The Divided Brain and the Making of the Western World*. London: Yale.

Meade, M. (1993). *Men and the Water of Life: Initiation and Tempering of Men*. San Francisco: Harper.

Meade, M. (2013). www.mosaicvoices.org/index.php?option=com content& view=category&layout=blog&id=42&Itemid=60. Last accessed 11 March 2014.

Mulhearn, A. (2012). *Healing Intelligence: The Spirit in Psychotherapy—Working With Darkness and Light*. London: Karnac.

Nutt, D. (2011). *Drugs Without the Hot Air*. Cambridge: UIT.

Nutt, D. (2013). "Financial crisis caused by too many bankers taking cocaine" says former drugs tsar. *Telegraph*, 16 April 2013. Available at www.telegraph.co.uk

Plato (1997). Timeaus. In: J. M. Cooper (Eds.), *Plato Complete Works*. D. J. Zeyl, Trans. Indianapolis: Hutchinson.

Rey, H. (1994). Further thoughts on "that which patients bring to analysis". *British Journal of Psychotherapy, 2*: 185–197.

Schore, A. (2012). *The Art and Science of Psychotherapy*. New York: Norton.

Some, M. (1993). *Ritual: Power, Healing and Community*. Oregon: Swan Raven.

Stanford encyclopedia of philosophy. (2013). www.plato.stanford.edu/entries/plato-timaeus/ Last accessed 11 March 2014.

Thompson, D. (2011). *The Fix*. London: Collins.

Van Kreiken, R. (1998). *Norbert Elias*. London: Routledge.

Wellings, N., & Wilde McCormick, E. (2000). *Transpersonal Psychotherapy: Theory and Practice*. London: Continuum.

Winnicott, D. W. (1960). Ego distortion in terms of true and false self. In: *The Maturational Processes and the Facilitating Environment: Studies in the Theory of Emotional Development* (pp. 140–152). London: Hogarth.

Winship, G. (2012). *Addictive Personalities and Why People Take Drugs*. London: Karnac.

Wright, J. (2005). *The Way Through the Wall*. J. Drew & D. Lorimer (Eds.). Lydney UK: First Stone.

Yates, P. R. (2013). www.medicine.manchester.ac.uk/healthmethodology/research/ndec/events/DrRowdyYates'presentation.pdf Last accessed 2013.

Zeyl, D. (2013). "Plato's Timaeus", *The Stanford Encyclopedia of Philosophy* (Spring 2013 Edition), Edward N. Zalta (Ed.), www.plato.stanford.edu/archives/spr2013/entries/plato-timaeus/ Last accessed 4 December 2013.

Zoja, L. (1989). *Drugs, Addiction and Initiation: The Modern Search for Ritual*. New York: Sligo Press.

CHAPTER THREE

The Self-Medication Hypothesis and attachment theory: pathways for understanding and ameliorating addictive suffering

The twentieth John Bowlby Memorial Lecture

Edward. J. Khantzian

Introduction

Our pejorative and unempathic attitude towards individuals labelled as having "Substance Use Disorders" (SUDs) in part derives from early psychoanalytic drive theory. Dual instinct theory suggested that addictive behaviour is driven by pleasure seeking or self-destructive motives, so much so that in the latter instance Menninger (1935) stated that addiction was suicide on an installment plan. What a misunderstanding. Our patients with "addictive disorders" are in need of being understood not so much as pleasure seekers or self-destructive characters, but more as individuals who are in pain and seek and need contact and comfort. The Self-Medication Hypothesis (SMH) derives from persistent clinical observation and inquiry about how individuals who depend on addictive substances do so because they have had the powerful discovery that what they suffer with is relieved temporarily by addictive substances. This is so whether it is a vague sense of dysphoria because feelings are confusing or elusive, or because affects are overwhelming and unbearable. Depending on the substance used, the psychoactive actions of the drugs of abuse provide short term surcease for a wide range of painful and confusing feeling states.

In this chapter I will briefly describe basic aspects of the Self-Medication Hypothesis. I will then review how it has stimulated a consideration of addiction as a self-regulation disorder, and to further consider how the suffering associated with addiction, especially traumatic suffering, disrupts the human capacity for secure attachments. I will use case material to provide examples of how these themes play out and are enacted in patients' lives and in the therapeutic relationship. Finally I will review how the Self-Medication Hypothesis and attachment paradigms, provide a basis to empathically and intersubjectively attune to and ameliorate the distress and suffering that drives addictive behaviour and relationships.

The self-medication hypothesis of addictive disorders

A fundamental premise of the SMH is that addiction behaviour is grounded in the human penchant (especially in the infant, but persisting into adulthood) for seeking comfort and contact, not pleasure. In this section I will review the elements of the SMH as first articulated (Khantzian, 1985), and subsequently elaborated upon (Khantzian, 1997). In the following section I will explain how my thinking evolved about the SMH to consider addiction as a self-regulation disorder (Khantzian, 2003).

In my early focus on self-medication factors in addictive disorders the main emphasis was on painful affect states which individuals were attempting to alleviate with addictive substances. My thinking at that time reflected the intersection of my psychodynamic/psychoanalytic training, which I was in the middle of, with the then evolving terminology for psychoactive drugs in general. Namely, starting in the early 1960s, we changed our terms for psychiatric medications from "tranquillizers" (i.e., major and minor tranquillizers) to designating them by their specific action (i.e., anti-psychotic, anti-anxiety, anti-depressant). My first systematic involvement with treating the addictions began with the initiation of the Methadone Maintenance Program at The Cambridge Hospital in 1970. Almost immediately I began to wonder what motivated the dependence on heroin. My thinking initially and subsequently reflected an evolution much like that with the change in nomenclature for prescribed psychotropic medications. I first speculated that heroin was a powerful opiate analgesic (i.e., a "pain killer") and that the appeal of the opiates resided in their ability to relieve emotional pain in general. Once I began evaluating each patient coming to the program, almost immediately I started to change my thinking, namely I began to consider that the effect of opiates had a more specific appeal. This change in thinking stimulated embryonic thinking about the SMH, as did the contributions of other psychodynamic investigators who coined the terms "drug-of-choice" (Weider & Kaplan, 1969) and "preferential use of drugs" (Milkman & Frosch, 1973).

The SMH proposes that addictive drugs have their appeal and become compelling principally for two reasons: first, they relieve human psychological suffering and, second, there is a considerable degree of specificity in a person's drug-of-choice. With regard to specificity, clinical experience reveals that individuals resort to more than one class of drugs, often a function of availability wherein they will juggle doses of other drugs to simulate their drug-of-choice, but when pursued more closely an individual will indicate a drug preference. The following is the description of the appeal of the main class of addictive drugs taken from the 1997 update of the SMH:

- Opiates. *Besides their general calming and "normalizing" effect, opiates attenuate intense, rageful, and violent affect. They counter the internally fragmenting and disorganizing effects of rage and the externally threatening and disruptive effects of such affects on interpersonal relations.*
- Central nervous system depressants (including alcohol). *Alcohol's appeal may reside in its properties as a "superego solvent". However, in my own experience, and based on observations by Krystal, short-acting depressants with rapid onset of action (e.g., alcohol, barbiturates, benzodiazepines) have their appeal because they are good "ego solvents." That is, they act on those parts of the self that are cut off from self and others by rigid defenses that produce feelings of isolation and emptiness and related tense/anxious states and mask fears of closeness and dependency. Although they are not good antidepressants, alcohol and related drugs create the illusion of relief because they temporarily soften rigid defenses and ameliorate states of isolation and emptiness that predispose to depression.*
- Stimulants. *Stimulants act as augmentors for hypomanic, high-energy individuals as well as persons with atypical bipolar disorder. They also appeal to people who are de-energized and bored, and to those who suffer from depression. In addition, stimulants, including cocaine, can act paradoxically to calm and counteract hyperactivity, emotional lability, and inattention in persons with attention-deficit/hyperactivity disorder (Khantzian, 1983, 1985).* (Khantzian, 1997, pp. 232–233)

Space consideration does not allow me to go into great detail here, but there are aspects of the SMH that are disputed and considered controversial. In the following section I will address some of these criticisms of and possible inconsistencies in the SMH. For example, some investigators support the concept of self-medication in addictive disorders, but questions the need for, or the validity of, the specificity issue (Darke, 2013), and others outright dismiss the SMH as dangerously false and misleading (DuPont & Gold, 2007).

I would mention here that the way I have garnered the specific appeal that patients experience with their drug-of-choice derives from a basic inquiry that I make and have made with each patient over the past four decades, namely, "What did the [preferred] drug do for you when you first used the drug?" Also, given the confusion and inaccessibility of feelings with which so many addicted individuals struggle, the specificity issues often becomes less clear. I have speculated elsewhere, how frequently the elusiveness and absence of feelings contributes to the repetitious, compulsive nature of addictive behaviour where the operative changes from the relief of suffering to the control of the suffering (Khantzian, 1995, 1997, 2003).

Addiction as a self-regulation disorder: trauma, attachment, and survival instincts

Criticisms of and seeming inconsistencies in the SMH stimulated me to begin to think about what else beyond painful or unmanageable affects are dysregulated in addictive behaviour and to consider addiction as a self-regulation disorder. However, before I get to those considerations, I would nevertheless emphasise the primary importance to affect life in relation to the addictions. Affects play an extremely important role in the development of addiction and cut across all other aspects of self-regulation. Affects are the organising basis for self-experience (Stolorow, Brandchaft, & Atwood, 1995), the foundation for a sense of wellbeing and self-esteem (Kohut, 1971, 1977), the currency for human connection and attachment (Bowlby, 1973), and a primary ingredient for guiding behaviour, especially self-care (Khantzian & Mack, 1983). Major trauma and neglect greatly heighten and worsen the self-regulation deficits that are so commonly and persistently associated with addictive disorders.

At least three factors stirred my consideration of addiction as a self-regulation disorder: first, many individuals suffer with painful emotional states and feelings but they do not necessarily become addicted; second, more often there are added painful affects that result as a consequence of addiction; and third, if the SMH suggests that addiction is an attempt at self-repair, how can all the associated self-harm, danger, and threat to life be explained? Because of space requirements I can only briefly summarise here how the deficits in self-regulation interact with each other and with addictive substances to make dependence more likely or compelling. The interested reader can find more detailed explanations elsewhere (Khantzian, 1985, 1995, 1997, 2003, 2012).

Addicted individuals suffer because they cannot regulate their emotions, self-other relations, and self-care. They self-medicate the pain and suffering associated with these self-regulation difficulties.

Patients with addictive disorders suffer in the extreme with their emotions. Feelings are cut-off, absent, or confusing, or they are intense and overwhelming. In the former case stimulating drugs can be enlivening or activating. If feelings are defensively restricted and cut-off, as they so often are in addicted people, the releasing properties of sedative-hypnotics in low to moderate doses can allow the experience and expression of feelings of warmth and closeness that they cannot otherwise allow. When feelings are threatening, or overwhelming, opiates can become captivating in their ability to powerfully contain intense, disorganising, and dysphoric affects, especially rage and associated agitation. Similarly, but not as effectively, high doses of depressants such as alcohol can contain such intense affect.

Shaky or poor sense of self/self-esteem and interpersonal relationships leave addictively prone individuals subject to discover the ameliorating effects of addictive substances and behaviours. Feelings of poor self cohesion and fragmentation are relieved by the calming action of opiates or sedatives in such individuals. The chronic absence of a sense of wellbeing and the inability to satisfactorily connect to others makes the soothing and comforting actions of opiates and depressants alluringly welcome. Narcissistic defenses of disdain and self-sufficiency related to poor self-esteem, which lead to feelings of isolation, are temporarily lifted in such individuals with stimulants or low to moderate doses of alcohol, and allow connection to others that otherwise would feel unallowable or undoable. For those who more passively resign themselves to withdraw with a sense of injured self, such a retreat is made easier with obliterating doses of alcohol.

Survival instincts in patients with addictive disorders are too often woefully underdeveloped or absent. In fact they are not instincts so much as developmental deficits in an (ego) capacity for self-care that assure survival. We have explored in more detail elsewhere (Khantzian & Mack, 1983; Khantzian, 1995, 1997, 2003, 2012) how in the absence or diminished capacities for self-care, addicted individuals fail to experience fear, worry, anticipatory shame, or alarm in the face of potential harm and danger, especially those associated with addiction. This deficit interacts malignantly with the pain and suffering involved with regulating emotions, self-esteem, and relationships to make addictive behaviour and attachment more likely. Furthermore, one has to feel worthy in order to take care of oneself, but meaningful and caring connections also help to assure wellbeing and safety.

I will be presenting three cases in this chapter.[1] In two of the three cases, addiction was not one of the looming issues, but as I indicate, it could have been. I use these cases, however, because they are most recent to the time of writing this chapter, and they robustly highlight the relational, intersubjective, and attachment themes central to this chapter and this conference. Furthermore, I hope it demonstrates how I try to attune and empathically work with the dysregulation and attachment issues with which my patients struggle.

The case that follows here highlights how major trauma and neglect in a person's early life can endlessly and repeatedly effect a person's sense of worthiness, self-esteem, and the inability to establish and maintain stable and comforting long-term relationships. Although the patient gives an indication how he might have become addictively attached to gambling, he was not addicted, but he could have been (subsequent to writing up this case I learned that both paternal grandparents were compulsive gamblers). His case also demonstrates an important corollary of the SMH, namely that addictive substances, albeit potentially and powerfully seductive, are not universally appealing for the majority of humans, and how and why this is so.

Jake

Jake is a fifty-seven-year-old admirable and dear person, this despite extraordinary abuse and abandonment at the hands of a cruel and alcoholic father, and traumatic withdrawal by his mother for a period when he was around five years old. He says that his mother withdrew from him at that time because she was a loving but misguided mother who worried that Jake would become a "momma's boy" after she divorced Jake's father. Walant (2002) would consider this kind of attitude as "normative abuse" wherein the need of the child for comfort and contact is subordinated to cultural norms. (In her 2002 publication she focused on how the child's needs are subordinated to separation and individuation consideration. More recently, she stresses how the child's needs are subordinated to a range of cultural assumptions because society holds those views as correct—personal communication.) Jake's trauma history was further compounded when at the age of nine he was sodomised, beaten, and threatened with his life if he told anyone. Significantly, and likely shaping an aspect of his personality organisation, he recalls that in that episode he survived by passively resigning to the beating and challenging the rapist to go ahead and beat him. Notwithstanding the trauma and neglect, he has experienced extraordinary accomplishments academically and professionally in his adult life, not without some painful setbacks. He is another one of the people with whom I have worked who could have become addicted but he had not, although in what follows he hinted that he could have succumbed to a behavioural or "process addiction." An unexpected developmental blessing and protection in this respect was the immersion in a rigorous academic programme in secondary school that initiated a life-long interest in the classics. It is likely that it contributed to and resonated with his intelligence which stimulated an enduring capacity to cerebrally and emotionally "mentalize" (Allen, Fonagy & Bateman, 2008) about life, factors all too often absent in addictively prone people.

After a manic episode in his mid-thirties wherein he erroneously mismanaged a client's fund as a Certified Public Accountant (CPA), he reinvented himself as an IT specialist working for various individuals and businesses as a very gifted and valued problem solver for all his clients. Married for about five years to a person that he felt was needy and whom he felt he could never satisfy, he divorced, but remained steadfastly devoted to his daughter. Subsequent to his divorce he periodically became involved in a number of relationships with women wherein he invariably promised and delivered more than he received and, more often, the relationships ended unsatisfactorily. In his business, he constantly displayed a tendency to under charge and to overextend himself in his dealings with his clients. A constant theme in his individual and group psychotherapy with me was the repetition to act as though undeserving and in ways not in his best interest. When pointed out, especially in group therapy, he would passively shrug his shoulders and say, "whatever."

In a recent psychotherapy visit he was lamenting that another IT person was vying for the business of one of his most valued and lucrative clients, a situation that was occurring at a time of decline in his business. He was complaining once again, as often happens, of feeling under appreciated and undervalued for the devotion he dedicated to his clients, not unlike how he often feels in his relations with his family. In this context he also shared a recent experience where he had similarly and mistakenly assumed his daughter was mad with him about a recent exchange. I said to him, "You feel like people who are supposed to love and take care of you keep fucking you over—that's your trauma experience speaking." He responded by reminding me that he has spent his whole life trying to please others at his own expense. Jake agreed with me when I said he was feeling it again with his client who might be unappreciatively switching the business to the new competitor.

As he was thinking out loud about some unsatisfactory alternatives of how to make up for lost income if he lost the client, I chose to address how I thought his trauma history was affecting his inability to renegotiate with the client. Namely to remind the client how diligently and conscientiously he did and could serve them and that he was in a better bargaining position than he could appreciate. I was subjectively responding to his feelings of under entitlement when he was describing his impulse to accede to the competitor when I somewhat playfully offered that I was having a "brilliant" insight (he had a wonderful sense of humour), namely I said, "What gets most damaged with a trauma history is survival instincts." He quickly affirmed my observation saying he's always put the interest of others ahead of his own.

After a pause I decided to ask him how come he had never become addicted. He explained he had tried a lot of drugs but thought his need to "keep [his] wits" about things and because of control issues, it had prevented his continued use. He said that was why he did not like marijuana. I also suspected that his otherwise dysfunctional and characteristic defense of passive resignation, in this respect, protected him from the more commonly observed risk taking associated with addictive behaviour. He added that he tried cocaine but that it did not do much for him and certainly it "was not a magical elixir". Jake also clarified that coming off cocaine he would get terribly depressed and weepy. Interestingly and significantly, he told me that when he was manic many years ago he drank two bottles of wine at a time to calm himself. At the end of the hour he thought out loud that he could have been an addictive gambler because he "could feel the rush" when he did gamble.

Jake was clear with me over the course of his therapy about how deeply he had suffered with his trauma. I was also aware how the consequences of the traumatic neglect and abuse weaved their way into the fabric of his personality organisation and profoundly played out around his self-care and interpersonal dealings. I was repeatedly impressed with how he had a tendency to get into numerous jams with promises that he made which he often could not adequately deliver on because he could be so overextended by them. I often felt he was extending to others what he wished had been extended to him during his traumatically damaging and depriving childhood. In this interview I thought the mini-crisis around losing a client evoked characteristic inhibitions and self-denial about his own needs. As I was experiencing his under entitlement it prompted me to respond by linking it to his trauma history. I believe that same subjective, or intersubjective, if you will, reaction was involved in my pursuing with him the almost invariable association that I and others have observed between Post-Traumatic Stress Disorder (PTSD) and addictive vulnerability. In this context with my addicted patients, I often light heartedly warn them about my "mother-hen instincts" when I wonder and worry with them about their behaviours; but I suspect it is an intersubjective response to the absent or inadequate hovering issues that they experienced when they were very young. It is also fair to say in Jake's case that he had a special "protection" against addictive vulnerability working for him; namely, to think and feel about the consequences of his drug experiences (i.e., "mentalize") and at least in this way, assured better self-care and welfare than he customarily allowed for himself. His reactions to my enquiry about addiction vulnerability was revealing and significant in that it affirmed once again that addictive substances for various reasons are not always captivating or universally appealing and that they can even be experienced as aversive. Whether it was intervening control issues or his passive resignation that protected him, or that he lacked a biological/genetic susceptibility, or other factors, was interesting and striking. Perhaps it was an indication that his keen intelligence and the capacity to make cause-consequence connections (invariably deficient in addictively prone individuals) served him to avoid the pitfall of addiction. Not insignificantly, he did self-medicate his dysphoria with large amounts of wine when he was manic, one more condition in which there is intense affect and agitation and a disproportionate association with substance dependence.

Frustrated attachment and self-medication

Attachment issues as Bowlby (1973) indicates persist from infancy through adult life. If humans are secure they proceed with a sense that they can engage and interact with others with a sense of comfort and confidence. When early attachments have been compromised, disrupted, traumatic, and neglectful, the human tendency is one of relational retreat and isolation and to attach to the inanimate dependencies of addictive substances and behaviours.

One can relate to some of this to the aphorisms that addicted patients adopt which reflects their conflict and ambivalence about their attachments:

> "We are relief seeking missiles"
> "We don't have relationships—we take hostages"
> Or as one patient put it, "I'm a born again isolationist"

Persuasive arguments have been advanced in the USA and the UK for conceptualising addiction as an attachment disorder. Walant (2002) places attachment issues at the root of addictive behaviour. She emphasises how parents place cultural norms for autonomy and individuation (and depending on the times, other cultural norms) ahead of the child's needs for closeness and dependency and thus there is a failure in empathic attunement to the child's attachment needs. For example, a chronically relapsing alcoholic patient recently recalled how when she was about eleven years old she remembers her mother insisting that they not hold her one-year-old brother when he cried because they would "spoil him". From Walant's perspective, substance dependent individuals need help psychotherapeutically in cultivating the capacity for attachment to counter the disengagement they have developed and adopted in childhood to avoid the pain of their interpersonal difficulties extending into adulthood. She describes necessary empathic, relational, and interactive approaches to psychotherapeutically achieve this end. Flores (2004) persuasively contends that establishing and maintaining solid attachment assures safety, human comfort, and wellbeing. He argues this is not just a good idea; it is the law. In the absence of solid attachments, alcoholism and addiction can result. On this basis he proposes that treatments targeting attachment dynamics through individual and group therapies are needed to challenge the counterdependency and interpersonal avoidances associated with substance use disorders.

In the UK, Reading (2002) has explored how the tenets of attachment theory are fundamental for understanding the relational deficits of people with an addiction and for unravelling the connections to their drug of choice. He places addiction in an interpersonal context and considers how individuals who might be addictively prone adopt the inanimate attachment to drugs to substitute for their inconsistent and insecure attachment issues that date back to their childhood. Reading (2002) elegantly proposes that client and therapist need to appreciate and understand together how "addictional bonds" (p. 23) replace affectional bonds.

The following case vignette illustrates how the problem of emotional reserve and inhibition dating back to childhood, interacting with contemporary issues of emotional disconnect with a spouse, fuelled a growing dependency on alcohol. It also illustrates how the therapeutic relationship can attune to and intersubjectively activate the issues of disconnection that compel addictive behaviour:

John

John is a fifty-one-year-old manager of a very successful family business (not his own) who can take much of the credit for its current achievements. He is a tall and proud man, and his bearing reflects his staunch, somewhat reserved puritanical heritage and values, although he is not without a sense of humour. His demeanour also reflected the family tendency to be reserved and unexpressive with emotions. I have been following him for about two-and-half years. He came under pressure from his wife who was experiencing his progressive heavy drinking as increasingly intolerable. He initially consented to weekly visits but shortly after achieving significant reduction in the amount and frequency of his drinking he indicated a preference to see me on a more intermittent but regular basis. Nevertheless, he said the visits were important because he felt I was an important "governing influence" in controlling his consumption of alcohol (a term he picked up from me upon which I will comment subsequently). Our relationship was supportive and friendly (at times even playful around our mutual interests in sports) but the visits were more in the nature of checkups on how he was controlling his use of alcohol, and how things were progressing at work and at home. We enjoyed a mutually respectful and admiring relationship. I appreciated his reluctance and inability to explore in more depth matters involving feelings and relationships, only periodically touching upon conflicts involving work related personnel encounters or issues in his family (his wife Jane tended to be socially isolated and recently was exhibiting some signs of depression). With the exception of a few relapses wherein his drinking was excessive and out of control, he was succeeding in limiting his drinking to one or two drinks or on rare occasions three drinks a day.

I am generally dogged with my patients in pursuing the issue of what their drug of choice does for them, that is, what are they self-medicating? It is an avenue to therapeutically access the distress that governs their use and overuse of substances, but it also plays an important part in establishing an empathic alliance. Namely, the approach shifts from a typical one in which the patient can feel scolded about what the drugs are doing *to* (italicised for emphasis) them, to one where an understanding is offered as to what the drug is doing *for* them. This is especially so given the harsh judgements that are placed on patients with an addiction for their drug use, not the least of which is the harsh judgements and shame patients place on themselves. I had only peripherally touched on the matter in my initial encounter with John and the best I could surmise with him was that it served the purpose of releasing him from his emotional and interpersonal reserve given his cultural background and moral rectitude.

> When we met this particular morning it was after my August break, and after several stops and starts working around his and my schedule. After reviewing a tense business negotiation that had caused him to miss our first scheduled visit after my vacation break, we touched on how things had been with his family. He spoke

glowingly of how his daughter and son were doing at college, but then more glumly spoke about how things were with him and his wife. Strikingly, I found a variation of a line from a Cole Porter tune going through my head, "I get a kick out of champagne". (Of course, and not insignificantly, in the song he doesn't get the kick out of champagne but he does get it with his woman.) At that point I thought to say, "So there's no spark there with Jane?" referring to her depressive anergia. He agreed and quickly acknowledged, when I suggested it, that it did explain how he could get the spark out of alcohol. After a pause, I asked him about their sexual life. He said there wasn't any, and furthermore, there hadn't been any for at least the past five years; and in fact it had waned dating back to the time after the children were born. John shared that his libido remained high but Jane seemed to have lost her sexual desire and they didn't talk about it. We quickly ascertained together that his excessive drinking and increasing time out of the house corresponded to the period of Jane's waning and absent interest in sexual contact. We continued with the "spark" metaphor, John indicating that lingering later at work or at the pub provided the spark he was missing at home. I wondered aloud if he had thought of getting the spark elsewhere, that is, relationally. He reminded me of his puritanical heritage and said that that would produce a crisis of conscience. I then somewhat cryptically asked him if he knew about oxytocin. I explained that it was the human hormone that is released with childbirth as well as with lovemaking, that it assures human bonding and intimacy. He quickly caught on that I was suggesting he was not only missing the spark that comes from relating sexually, but also the spark that comes with intimate human connection and comfort. I wondered with him how he was dealing with less spark coming from "champagne" and might he be subject to relapse with alcohol excess or some other excess. As the end of the hour neared, he rather sheepishly shared with me that he enjoyed the company of a very attractive, single woman, Susan, on the occasion of business meetings and social functions, quickly inserting that it was a friendship he much enjoyed, but that it was not sexual. When asked if keeping a secret like that was not a source of conflict and guilt, he assured me that his wife Jane knew Susan and more often John would mention that he would be attending a meeting or event with her to which she did not object. He ended by saying, "So how could I feel guilty if Jane knew?"

Speaking intersubjectively, from somewhere in my psyche and that of John's and with the help of Cole Porter, the word "spark" jumped into my consciousness and into our interaction. It stimulated an inroad into and a better understanding of the emotional and relational vacuum with which John lived at home. It also gave me insight into what he was actually self-medicating. Given his reserve and Jane's depressive anergia, disconnection, and disinterest in their relationship, it provided John and I with a basis to appreciate how and why these factors had interacted such that he had progressively depended on alcohol and found its effect increasingly appealing. That appreciation also provided us with a basis to explore an aspect of his personal life that was close, meaningful, and enriching, which he had not shared with anybody. I felt, and he gave some indication going out the door, that he felt similarly; namely that he and I were now better connected around what alcohol did for him, as well as understanding the very important relationship with Susan. It provided us with a better relational vehicle to continue to monitor what his use of alcohol meant, and for he and I to better appreciate his need for human warmth and connection. Finally, we have reviewed elsewhere how "self-governance", alluded to earlier by John and I in our session, is not a one person psychology; that solving alcohol problems, and life problems in general, are best not solved alone but in a self-other, interpersonal context (Khantzian & Mack, 1989).

Disordered self-regulation, trauma, and the incapacity for secure attachments

In what follows I will, from a self-medication and attachment perspective, review how traumatic life experiences, whether they be abusive or neglectful, profoundly affect the human capacity for self-regulation. I will in particular stress how developmental disturbances in affect life and the impact on sense of self and self-esteem powerfully interact to derail the capacity for secure, trusting, and comforting relationships and thus make it more likely that individuals will turn to and find comfort and relief in addictive substances. As Reading (2002) and others have stressed, and as a central tenet of this chapter, when attachments are troubled, individuals often substitute chemical connections for human ones.

Substance dependent individuals become powerfully attached to their drugs because they have discovered that short term addictive drugs work. They can relieve the suffering associated with feelings that are confusing and absent, or feelings that are intense and overwhelming. If feelings are on shutdown there's no impetus to connect; if feelings are too intense and overwhelming they threaten self and relationships with others. These basic problems with affect regulation are important because, from the earliest phases of development, affects are the principal organisers of self-experience throughout life (Stolorow, Brandchaft & Atwood, 1995). It is the view of Stolorow and his colleagues that the function of "self objects" fundamentally refers "to the integration of affect into the organization of self-experience" (Stolorow, Brandchaft & Atwood, 1995, p. 66). This idea underscores the importance of the need for attuned responsiveness to affect states in all stages of life, attunement that tragically has been insufficient or absent in individuals with insecure attachment patterns that may lead to addictive behaviours. This has obvious clinical implications for empathic attunement to the developmental incapacities we encounter and for us as therapists to know, experience, and verbalise feelings with which addictively prone individuals suffer.

Discussing the role of affects in the development of our sense of self, Stolorow and associates emphasise the role of parental responsiveness and when it has not been steady and attuned, self-fragmentation results. "Defenses against affect then become necessary to preserve the integrity of a brittle self-structure" (Stolorow, Brandchaft & Atwood, 1995, p. 67). Substance use is not considered by Stolorow and colleagues here, but it could have been, namely substance dependent individuals suffer because they lack in experiences of inner comfort, coherence and constancy, and addictive substances, especially the more calming and soothing ones, serve that purpose. The impoverished sense of self, so commonly evident with individuals who have an addiction, also significantly contributes to poor self-esteem and lack of mature self-love such as self-respect and pride. In their absence, meaningful and trusting connections to others are unlikely. In this respect, the activating and stimulating action of drugs such as cocaine or crystal meth help such individuals break through their impoverished or diminished sense of self to "connect to others", otherwise they are unable to. However, stimulant users speak of the pseudo-intimacy the drug provides, referring to such interactions as "speed talk".

The following two vignettes involving a patient I shall call Kate, embody how growing up in a traumatising and neglectful home environment left her with a lifelong sense of feeling undervalued, lonely, and unimportant. The vignettes also provide a chance to see how these dynamics can become activated, enacted in the treatment relationship, and therapeutically joined in treatment.

Kate, Thursday 18 October 2012

Before I get to Kate, I share a vignette a supervisor shared with me a long time ago. It goes something like this:

> Patient comes into the psychiatrist's office feeling awful; the psychotherapist feels okay. The session ends, the patient walks out the door feeling better; the psychiatrist feels awful. Something went wrong.

It worked differently with Kate and me when we met today for her weekly psychotherapy which I will explain shortly.

Kate has suffered unimaginable painful, crippling and disfiguring arthritis affecting all her joints, extremities, hips, and her spine. She is not addicted, but she is drug dependent. I will explain the difference subsequently. Her high doses of opiate analgesics for her pain have likely kept her chronic anger, if not rage, at tolerable levels intrapsychically and interpersonally. She has had a series of therapies with me dating back over thirty years. When I first met her she reminded me of a beautiful variation of Barbara Streisand. Needless to say she appears quite differently now. Her life and pain has been further complicated and compounded by a life threatening condition her daughter has suffered since childhood; it involves a rare circulatory condition wherein any injury or infection to her upper extremities could become a catastrophic fatal event. Kate is a physician assistant and to her credit and dismay she more often knows what is in her daughter's best interest, better than the clinicians who encounter her when there is one of the many and recurrent crises with her condition.

Kate's mother suffered from the consequences of both parents being alcoholics rendering Kate's mother unempathic and emotionally unavailable to Kate in her years of growing up. In addition to the effects of witnessing violent and abusive interactions between her parents, and painful spankings when mother or father were in a bad mood, the main effect of the traumatic neglect in Kate's life has been to make her adapt by becoming a selfless person, subordinating her needs in general, but particularly to the needs and care of her chronically ill daughter, an athletic son, and an anxious husband. In the case of her husband Tom, his anxiety drove him to succeed in his career as a trial lawyer and to be seemingly oblivious to Kate's suffering and all the challenges she faces in managing their home, to say nothing of all the additional burdens of their daughter's medical conditions. The central theme for our current psychotherapeutic work has involved helping Kate to feel validated and supported around the deep bitter resentment and rage that has accumulated over the years towards her husband's unavailability, at the same time trying to help her appreciate how the intensity of her reactions is fuelled and amplified because of painful, enduring feelings of abandonment and neglect by her mother.

I say Kate could have become addicted because the intensity of her physical and emotional pain is so profound, affecting all aspects of her life and in particular, her self-esteem and relationships. Had she experimented with addictive drugs she might have become hooked on one of them. It could have been the ameliorating action of an opiate, especially the potentially calming and muting effect of heroin on her bitter resentment and rage; or it could have been the stimulating/activating action of cocaine that might have countered her despair and anhedonia. Is this not the flip-flop of affective numbing and flooding of PTSD? I offer a snippet of an interaction between us today that typifies, notwithstanding her husband's neglect, how unworthy she feels in general and acts around any source of comfort and acceptance of her distress and pain.

> On this particular day I was no less awed by how deep and pervasive her suffering is as she was characteristically reviewing past and present hurts and resentments, as usual, mostly targeting her husband. Then at one point as the end of the hour neared, she in passing mentioned that she had experienced a new pain this past week in her left groin area. When I asked her to elaborate about it she brushed me off with in effect an "oh well" reaction, almost as if I wouldn't be interested. I quickly pointed out, "As soon as you told me about your pain you dismissed me". Somewhat sarcastically she replied, "What about my pain do you want me to talk about?" I simply suggested she should talk with me more about her pain, reminding her that with her background as a child she had

never developed that kind of a voice or felt worthy of attention. Welling up with bitter tears she said, "It's a lot … it keeps me from feeling I have a purpose in life … it limits me, I can't go out and do what I want to do." I told her that that's what she should be talking about. She again reverted to directing her resentment towards her husband, but this time with a different and, literally, a louder voice, "I want him to feel, he doesn't feel, [and even more loudly] … just feel!" As we were both standing, and as she was about to go out of the door, with bitter deep sadness and crying, I thought to re-remind her that she had almost dismissed me today about her groin pain. I offered, "Maybe today going out the door, hopefully with less pain, you might let me feel it." She thanked me as she opened the door and left.

We often at times like these, when we witness compounding tragedy and loss such as Kate's, find ourselves thinking, "This is like pages out of Job (the old testament prophet)." There has been no exception for me with Kate in this respect. Her life has involved tragic developmental traumatic neglect and abuse culminating in the marriage to an anxious man who could not get beyond his own problems to properly respond to those of his wife, and then the major near unbearable medical conditions that she and her daughter have endured. Working and staying with the intensity and depth of her suffering has been one of the most difficult clinical challenges in my career. To my understanding, what has mattered the most in her case has been staying with her pain. Some might wonder, as my opening vignette suggests, that Kate was dumping her emotions on me. An intersubjective perspective would suggest otherwise. Our work together suggested to me the need for more corrective and, hopefully, transformative interactions. Such interactions, as she evoked with me this day, might over time allow for the lessening of Kate's suffering through processes of empathic acceptance of her pain and to help her to feel freer of the toxic resentments. At the same time gentle forays into Kate's characteristic defenses can help her better appreciate how she unwittingly fosters her worst dilemma of feeling no one can accept or understand how she feels, a dilemma that fuels and heightens her bitterness and rage. As the mentalizing and intersubjective theorists suggest (Allen, Fonagy & Bateman, 2008; Stolorow, Brandchaft & Atwood, 1995), a secure therapeutic attachment can serve to reignite, activate, and promote hope and trust that was lost or absent in childhood. I can concur with them that human relationships, starting with me as her therapist and her first experience of a secure enough base, can supplant conscious and unconscious defenses and resistances against meaningful and comforting relationships.

Kate—15 November 2012

This morning I was reminded about the difference between being "addicted" and being "drug dependent", namely, in the case of the former, addicted means a person is drug dependent, but additionally they are continuously drug seeking, using without medical supervision, and using in a way that is harmful and dangerous, and use is continued despite all the negative consequences. Drug dependent simply means that one is physiologically dependent and if drug use is stopped abruptly the individual experiences painful physical withdrawal symptoms.

This morning in the context of my being interrupted by a call about another patient needing Suboxone to detoxify from opiates, a brief exchange followed with Kate about how she is prescribed a moderately high dose of long acting oxycodone four times per day to manage the crippling arthritic pain. So she is drug dependent. She admits she experiences withdrawal symptoms and pain if she cuts back or does not take the oxycodone.

But that's not what was significant about this morning's visit. Or was it? Because it was about pain—her pain and mine. Shortly after the interruption with my call and our exchange about her dependence on the pain medication, and one more diatribe about how disconnected her husband is about her needs and isolation, we were again interrupted when her daughter rang her twice on her mobile phone and she chose to take the call on the second ring. It was absolutely striking to me the marked change in her demeanour and her animated and affectionate and loving tone with her daughter. After she hung up in a rather loud and impassioned way I exclaimed, "My God Kate! You so much need to be in a loving place … it might be a Herculean challenge, but you need to find a way to love Tom."

After stressing to her how much more comfortable she appeared as she lovingly spoke with her daughter, I emphatically affirmed,

"Kate, please appreciate that although I am raising my voice, know that I am on your side." She responded impassively, "That very astute." "Are you being sarcastic?" I asked. The answer was, "Yes". I was enraged and wanted to say, "How dare you!" Instead I protested loudly, candidly indicating to her that I experienced and was with her pain more than I had ever been with any patient. But then I added that she can't fix Tom's abominable and disappointing ways but she needs to see how she thrives when feeling loving, but dies emotionally when she remains bitterly cynical and cut-off. To my total surprise, going out of the door she responded, saying that she had an "attitude problem".

From an intersubjective perspective, I realise my anger/rage with her (acted on and expressed) kept me in the room with her, and her reactions to me, came together to benefit her therapeutically. Maybe it was materially important for her to gather in my reaction subjectively and it played a part in examining and better appreciating her "attitude problem."

Therapeutic implications[2]

As we have indicated, individuals who have become dependent on addictive drugs suffer because they are overwhelmed by or cut-off from their feelings, their sense of self and self-esteem is precarious, their capacity for secure attachments and comfortable relationships are elusive, and self-care is underdeveloped. Therapists and patients need to work together to access and understand how these vulnerabilities are intimately involved in the development of a dependency on addictive substances and other repetitive self-defeating behaviours. In this concluding section I will highlight some of the necessary elements and therapeutic modes of interaction for effective psychotherapeutic action.

Psychoanalytic approaches of passivity, therapeutic detachment, and strictly interpretive techniques, are not best suited for individuals with addictive disorders if they are suited at all, and more likely such approaches perpetuate the confusion, shame, sense of alienation, and disconnection with which patients with an addiction suffer. In my work I have emphasised the need to be more interactive (balance talking and listening), and incorporate attitudes of kindness, support, empathy, respect, patience, and instruction in the service of building and maintaining a strong therapeutic alliance and attachment. These elements are essential in order to deal with and overcome the problems with self-regulation, which we have previously reviewed in this chapter, that become so powerfully linked to addictive behaviors (Khantzian, 2012–2013).

When patients seem confused and say they do not know what they are feeling, therapists can help by evoking, identifying, and putting into words, feelings as they surface or become apparent in the therapeutic interactions. Instruction is often a necessary mode in this respect and entirely consistent with a psychodynamic approach. This is where the emphasis on "mentalizing" is so germane to work with people who have problems with an addiction. For those who suffer with intense and unbearable affect, it is worth remembering how the therapeutic relationship itself is a containing influence when such intense emotions are met with patience, forbearance, and respect for the origins of such distressful states. Otherwise patient and therapist withdraw from each other and the connection and attachment problems are repeated in the therapy relationship. Clearly such intensity of affect is one of the main and most troubling consequences of PTSD. The legitimacy of such reactions needs to be appreciated and acknowledged and the process of linking such rage and anger to the person's need to resort to addictive substances helps patients to feel understood and validated. Gentle explorations of the experiences that engender such emotions can gradually diminish or resolve such intense affect. In this context, judicious use of legitimate psychotropic medications targeting these affects can significantly attenuate the intensity to make the working through of these affects in psychotherapy more possible.

It is in the realm of a shaky sense of self and the relational difficulties of patients with an addiction that the importance of kindness, empathy, and support provide effective attunement to their needs for appreciation and validation, and how their injured sense of self and their relational distrusts and dis-ease leave them so susceptible to the inanimate attachment to addictive substances. Individuals with an addiction feel undeserving of the care and connection to others. Being interactive, engaging, and empathic are important elements in responding to patients' ambivalence about relationships. Impassivity and detached interpretations can be countertherapeutic and re-traumatising. Careful exploration of the ambivalence about relationships can materially stimulate possibilities of beneficial connections to others. It is in this respect that the connections stimulated by individual and group therapy, and Twelve-step programmes are extraordinarily helpful in addressing and ameliorating the attachment difficulties and sense of alienation with which substance dependent individuals struggle (Khantzian, 2013).

The unthinking and unfeeling behaviours of patients who are substance dependent that are characteristic of deficits in self-care become evident in the therapeutic relationship through the alarm stirred up in the therapist by a patient's risky or dangerous behaviour. Such reactions and interactions can alert the therapist and patient to how such deficits are major factors in relapse. As we have indicated, patients benefit from realising how more often such deficits derive from traumatic and neglectful environments that leave them ill-prepared in assuring their well-being and safety. When therapists witness these deficits they should be unhesitant in using their reactions of alarm and concern that patients stir to identify the lack of such responses in the patient. Constant attention to patients' poor self-care can help to instill a growing awareness of how their self-care deficits continuously leave those so affected continuously in harm's way, especially those involved with the harm and dangers associated with addictive substances. Long term therapy often helps in reaching and understanding the developmental and environmental roots of these deficits, but a here-and-now, active, instructive approach is essential in order to stimulate and enable a better capacity to recognise, anticipate, and avoid self-harm, particularly related to addictive substances. "We need to help patients use self-respect, feelings of apprehension/worry, relationships with others, and thoughtfulness as a guide for safe behavior and self-preservation" (Khantzian, 2012, p. 278).

In conclusion, a contemporary psychoanalytic understanding of addiction has generated and documented observable, developmental, structural, ego/self, and relational disturbances that predispose a person to maintain addictive behaviours and the accompanying insecure attachment relationships. These findings provide a basis to guide therapists in focusing on the self-regulation problems of patients with an addiction psychotherapeutically. Impassive and strictly interpretive approaches are contraindicated if not outright damaging. Modern psychotherapeutic practice employs more relational, interactive, supportive, and empathic attitudes and approaches to help patients and therapists to focus on the vulnerabilities and dysfunction that perpetuate addictive suffering and pain. This contemporary attachment and relational perspective provides understanding, hope, and more effective means to overcome the compelling, self-defeating, and tragic causes and consequences of addiction (Khantzian, 2013).

Notes

1. The identity of the cases have been disguised to preserve patient anonymity.
2. This final section is based on two recent publications (Khantzian, 2012–2013).

References

Allen, J. G., Fonagy, P., & Bateman, A. W. (2008). *Mentalizing in Clinical Practice*. Washington, DC: American Psychiatric Publishing.

Bowlby, J. (1973). *Attachment and Loss: Volume 2. Separation: Anxiety and Anger*. New York: Basic Books.

Darke, S. (2013). Pathways to heroin dependence: time to reappraise self-medication. *Addiction, 108*: 659–667.

DuPont, R. L., & Gold, M. S. (2007). Comorbidity and "Self-Medication". *Journal of Addictive Disorders, 26*, 1: 13–23.

Flores, P. J. (2004). *Addiction as an Attachment Disorder*. New York: Jason Aronson.

Khantzian, E. J. (1985). The self-medication hypothesis of addictive disorders. *American Journal of Psychiatry, 142*: 1259–1264.

Khantzian, E. J. (1995). Self-regulation vulnerabilities in substance abusers: Treatment implications. In: S. Dowling (Ed.), *The Psychology And Treatment Of Addictive Behavior* (pp. 17–41). New York: International Universities Press.

Khantzian, E. J. (1997). The self-medication hypothesis of substance use disorders: A reconsideration and recent applications. *Harvard Review of Psychiatry, 4*: 231–244.

Khantzian, E. J. (2003). Understanding addictive vulnerability: An evolving psychodynamic perspective. *Neuro-Psychoanalysis, 5*: 5–21.

Khantzian, E. J. (2012). Reflections on treating addictive disorders: A psychodynamic perspective. *The American Journal on Addictions, 21*: 274–279.

Khantzian, E. J. (2013). Psychodynamic psychotherapy for the treatment of substance use disorders. In: N. El-Guebaly, M. Galanter, & G. Carra, (Eds.), *The Textbook of Addiction Treatment: International Perspectives*. In press; New York: Springer.

Khantzian, E. J. & Mack, J. E. (1983). Self-preservation and the care of the self: Ego instincts reconsidered. *Psychoanalytic Study of the Child, 38*: 209–232.

Khantzian, E. J. & Mack, J. E. (1989). Alcoholics Anonymous and contemporary psychodynamic theory. In: M. Galanter (Ed.), *Recent Developments in Alcoholism* (pp. 67–89). New York: Plenum.

Kohut, H. (1971). *The Analysis of the Self.* New York: International Universities Press.

Kohut, H. (1977). *The Restoration of the Self.* New York: International Universities Press.

Menninger, K. (1938). *Man Against Himself.* New York: Free Press.

Milkman, H., & Frosch, W. A. (1973). On the preferential abuse of heroin and amphetamine. *Journal of Nervous and Mental Disease, 156*: 242–248.

Reading, B. (2002). The application of Bowlby's attachment theory to the psychotherapy of the addictions. In: M. Weegmann & R. Cohen (Eds.), *The Psychodynamics of Addiction* (p. 23). London: Whurr.

Stolorow, R. D., Brandchaft, B., & Atwood, G. E. (1995). *Psychoanalytic Treatment: An Intersubjective Approach.* London: Routledge.

Walant, K. B. (2002). *Creating the Capacity for Attachment: Treating Addictions and the Alienated Self.* New York: Jason Aronson.

Weider, H., & Kaplan, E. (1969). Drug use in adolescents. *Psychoanalytic Study of the Child, 24*: 399–431.

CHAPTER FOUR

Alcohol misuse, attachment dilemmas, and triangles of interaction: a systemic approach to practice

Arlene Vetere

> For not only young children, it is now clear, but human beings of all ages are found to be at their happiest and to be able to deploy their talents to best advantage when they are confident that, standing behind them are one or more trusted persons who will come to their aid should difficulties arise. The person trusted provides a secure base from which his (or her) companion can operate.
>
> —Bowlby, 1973, p. 407

Attachment theory: implications for systemic therapy

Attachment theory has many important and helpful implications for therapeutic practice with individuals, couples, and families where alcohol misuse is the focus of concern, and not least, because attachment theory conceptualises heavy drinking as a problem of affect regulation. Attachments are considered to be representational, about caregiving, comfort, and affection, and in adult relationships, about sexuality. Attachment theory does not pathologise dependency in our relationships with key attachment figures, rather seeing autonomy and effective dependency as different sides of the same attachment coin. In this chapter, I shall explore the weave of attachment theory with systemic thinking and practice to consider how a person might come to rely on alcohol before people, and to trust alcohol to "look after them" more reliably than any person could or might (Dallos & Vetere, 2009).

Systemic interventions are like process consultations. We help people identify difficult and unhelpful patterns of interaction, so that they might better predict, de-escalate and then prevent them in favour of developing more satisfying patterns that promote accessible and responsive interactions. Attachment theory brings a theory of love to our understanding of our intimate relationships, and our need for closeness, comfort, and belonging. This understanding helps illuminate the unspoken attachment longings in our relationships with intimate family members, which if left unspoken, can lead to patterns of disappointment, emotional distancing, or critical pursuit. Attachment theory, though, has mostly developed in the context of dyadic relationship understandings, whereas systemic analysis has focused on triangular relationships as a minimum of understanding. For example, when any two meet and interact, their relationship and responsiveness to each other is influenced by their relationship with a "third", who may be absent, or dead. For example, a child's relationship with her mother is influenced by both their relationships with the child's father; a couple's relationship is influenced by both their relationship with a respective parent; or a couple's relationship is influenced by both their relationship with the alcohol bottle, and so on.

Thus the implications of attachment theory for systemic therapeutic practice with couples and families include the following:

a. helping family members name their emotional experience, explore the relational meaning of emotions and to better regulate their affective experience and interactions;

b. to promote curiosity and empathic appreciation of the emotional experience of the "other", which is never easy when we are unhelpfully emotionally aroused ourselves!

c. to promote the capacity for self-soothing and the seeking, giving, and receiving of comfort in a context of a new sense of entitlement to be looked after;

d. to enable calmer more reflective information processing during difficult moments in our interactions with our loved ones—never easy when our own unhelpful physiological arousal preoccupies us!; and

e. to help us integrate across our different representational systems and transform them by learning to give a good account of ourselves and others.

If one of the purposes of therapeutic intervention is to help us co-create narratives of healing in our relationships, we need to be able to harness and use all our memory resources. Attachment representations are layered and it is believed they are held in different memory systems, that is, procedural memory, sensory memory, semantic memory, episodic memory, and integrative memory (Tulving, 1983). Arguably, all the major psychotherapies aim to promote the integration of emotion, thought, and action through the development of our reflective capacities, for example, meta-cognition, meta-communication, or reflective self-functioning.

Family systems theory

Pattern in communication

Alcohol may be used to regulate emotional experience, to soothe and relax, and at the extremes, may be used to "numb out" and emotionally anaesthetise, blocking out unbearable feelings of guilt, sadness, fear, and shame. This may have been the reason for starting to consume alcohol or may be the ironic consequence of social consumption. Growing up in a family context where people may not be trusted, and where children have not been taught to self-soothe, the potential to rely on alcohol becomes much greater. In daily family life there may be differences in emotional expression and talk about feelings depending on whether family members, such as parents, are sober or inebriated. For children this can create confusion, uncertainty, and unpredictability, particularly if there is no one to help them understand what is happening, and to make sense of their different experiences with a sober or drinking parent. When couples and families come into therapy because their loved one is drinking heavily, they may well accuse them of telling lies about how much they drink, when they drink, or where they have hidden the drink. Family members can become the best detectives in searching out "the truth". In these circumstances, family members who drink may well feel blamed and shamed and this in turn, may make it more likely they turn again to alcohol to soothe themselves. Non-drinking family members may feel embarrassed or shamed in public by the drinking partner's behaviour and thus may increase their efforts to shame the drinker in the hope this may make them stop. In therapy it is helpful to reframe "telling lies" as needing to "talk straight" in an effort to promote clear, direct, and straightforward communication about what is happening, what is being experienced, and the hopes and fears for the present and the future (Vetere & Henley, 2001).

Pattern in relationships

Systemic theory conceptualises the development of patterns in our relationships, that is, repeated, predictable cycles of interaction that family members experience as more or less satisfying, more or less bonding, and more or less productive. When there are high levels of concern, anxiety, stress, and uncertainty within the family, problem drinking as a solution to the stress is likely to become more entrenched. Under these circumstances, extremes of responding can develop, such as symmetrical patterns of escalation or more complementary, constraining patterns of interaction. Reciprocity in relationships is harder to achieve under these conditions. Issues of power and control come to dominate, either in an escalating competitive pattern or in a dominant-submissive complementary pattern. Either way, family members often report feeling "stuck" and helpless in their experience of repeating the same cycles without clear solutions in sight. When anxiety levels are high, we are more likely to fall back on "old" solutions, and repeat them, even when we know they are not effective. For example, imagine a couple called Pete and Mary. Pete has a tendency to be preoccupied when he fears attachment threat, and Mary has a tendency to deactivate, and downregulate her arousal in difficult moments. Mary comes home from work one evening. Her day was difficult, she is tired and wants to spend the evening sitting on the sofa watching television. She does not tell Pete about her bad day. Pete notices that Mary looks tired and wants to help her. He suggests they go out for dinner so they do not need to cook. Mary says she is too tired and becomes irritated with Pete for suggesting they go out as it involves effort, effort to get ready, and so on. Pete feels hurt that Mary has so quickly dismissed his suggestion to go out. He becomes physiologically aroused and pursues Mary by suggesting again that they go out. Mary feels further irritated that Pete seems not to be listening to her and once again turns down his offer, saying she is tired. She begins to feel imposed on, and as the pattern repeats she begins to feel suffocated. Pete, on the other hand, feels hurt and rejected and in the context of his escalating unhelpful arousal pursues Mary for reassurance. We might ask, who takes the first drink? What if they both drink alcohol? What if the pattern persists whilst drinking, could the unhelpful escalation continue?

Therapy in this context, works to identify the unhelpful patterns, whether implicated in the drinking or not, and attempts to externalise the pattern as the problem to be solved, and to reduce the sense of blame and shame, which is so paralysing for some people. Family members' "internal working models" of whether they, or others, are deserving of attention and worthy of care can become activated. Therapists work "within" and "between" in these moments, carefully tracking the interplay of our beliefs about ourselves and others and how they are actualised in behaviour patterns during difficult moments of attachment threat or attachment injury. If and when the problem drinking ends, the therapist can help the family members navigate the impact of stopping the drinking. This is often a time when couples "go to the wire" and consider whether they wish to remain together. The stress of coping with long term drinking can leave little energy and mental space to consider life alternatives, but once released from the constant threat of heavy drinking, and with time to reflect on a history of negative projections and negative transference, some couples will decide to separate. A safe separation between a couple, especially when children are involved, can be a positive outcome.

Pattern over time and life cycle issues

The outcome research on family involvement in therapy for drinking problems suggests families are most helpful in motivating the drinker into treatment and in supporting the drinker in recovery (O'Farrell & Fals-Stewart, 2002). This research sees families as resourceful and supports the idea of the family as part of the solution. So, when a couple or family come into therapy, seeking help to stop the drinking, we ask "why now?" Often it can be a period of transition that prompts entry into treatment, when adaptation is needed for a predictable life event, such as the birth of a child, or in managing an unexpected crisis or life event (Carter & McGoldrick, 1988). Transitions are opportunities for change and can be used to develop new responses, or generative scripts. Our beliefs and constructs tend to be less fixed at a time of crisis, and more malleable to scrutiny and open for change. It is always helpful to ask about how the decision to come into treatment was taken, and what has changed in family relationships since the decision, as these self-observations often contain the seeds of future solutions.

When problem drinking has endured for years, families can become problem determined systems (Anderson, Goolishian & Winderman, 1986). This is the idea that family life becomes organised around the drinker and the problem of drinking, rather than being organised around the needs of all family members. This is seen as an ironic consequence of trying to manage and adapt to drinking problems and the impact on family life. For example, heavy drinking is known to be associated with physical health problems, violence in relationships, vulnerability to depression, anxiety and suicide, difficulties at work, unemployment, financial problems, public disorder, and impacts on children's development. Therapy helps the family to rebalance, to reconfigure roles and responsibilities, and to resume routines and rituals without fear of drinking. For example, children may have adopted parental roles, helping to manage the household and younger children. Whist such involvement develops compassion and social competence in children, it can also make demands on them beyond their capacity to cope, both emotionally and physically.

The "relationship to help" (Reder & Fredman, 1996) describes beliefs held in the family about when and how to involve outsiders in helping to solve family problems. At times of family difficulty, safety and protection are paramount. So, for example, if members of a family have learned to deactivate emotional arousal in the face of attachment threat (a dismissing strategy), or that others are not to be trusted because they only disappoint, family members may delay seeking help, or not seek help at all until the difficulties are severe and entrenched. They may hold a belief that it is shameful to seek outside help and thus expose inner sources of shame. In contrast, if family members struggle to regulate their arousal (a preoccupied strategy) and live with constant or unpredictable threats of emotional rejection and abandonment, they may well involve numerous people in helping them or make demands on others to solve their problems. Living in a context of chronic and unresolved high arousal makes it harder to think clearly and reflectively, and under conditions of threat, explanations may be simplified as a way of coping, along with a tendency to blame others. Thus engagement is crucial.

Engagement

If a family member or a partner has developed a primary attachment to alcohol, then any therapy could be seen as a threat, and particularly a relationship therapy, that might imply having to face the disappointment and resentment of others. In our experience the role of the alcohol key worker is crucial in forming a bridge between ourselves as systemic therapists and the person with the drinking problem. Alcohol key workers may well be the first people that those with a drinking problem come to trust, the first with whom they take the emotional risk of engagement. Thus we form a therapeutic triangle with the alcohol key worker, and the drinker, within which the alcohol key worker helps to stabilise the triangle. We find it helpful to offer consultation with our systemic therapy team first, as much as is needed, a form of putting one's toe in the water to feel the temperature. This brief and repeated exposure to us affords the opportunity to get to know us, and the ways in which we think and work, before making a commitment to a therapeutic process. Our accessibility and responsiveness during the consultation period builds a secure base within which containment, emotional safety, relational risk taking, comfort, and reflection can be both encouraged and developed. Empathy in the therapeutic alliance can involve reaffirming and clarifying clients' experiences and modelling understanding and acceptance for all family members. The pace can be slowed so that difficult and painful memories can be processed. Comfort may be offered to support clients in this work, whilst helping them explore and develop new meanings for their profound emotional experiences, past and present. This enables clarity and coherence in narrative skill and integration across all representational memory systems.

Attachment strategies

Attachment strategies for regulating emotional arousal are conceptualised on a continuum as styles of protective and defensive processes (Crittenden, 2006). These preferred strategies for regulating unhelpful arousal are thought to be activated by the perception of danger, which usually takes the form of an attachment threat, that is, a fear of rejection or abandonment, or an attempt to humiliate. They develop in the context of early experiences of being looked after. For example, if children learn that their expressions of distress do not elicit comfort or caring, they may develop a defensive strategy of dismissing or excluding certain emotions and experiences. Cognition can be relied on to help them inhibit affect and deny physiological discomfort and the need for others, such that they put effort into persuading themselves they are alright. Alcohol use can function to relax and comfort when others are not available or not seen as potentially helpful and lead to a form of reliance that supports no change. At the other end of this continuum is a preoccupied strategy that develops in a context of unpredictable caretaking. When children cannot predict the response from their carer other than knowing that sometimes their carer is warm and responsive, they may develop coercive and clinging strategies designed to elicit the desired response. This inability to predict causes confusion and leads to chronic over arousal, so that the child may rely more on affective information. Complexity may be reduced by oversimplifying and blaming others. Anger may be shown and used to elicit a carer's attention such that the anxiety and vulnerability beneath it remain hidden. Alcohol may have been used in the child's family of origin as a way of managing emotional experience, or may have been introduced during peer group experimentation. Alcohol can play a powerful role in down regulating chronic over arousal. Dismissing and preoccupied strategies may be reinforced over time and continue into adulthood if other more satisfying and protective relationships are unable to develop at the same time.

In contrast to these protective strategies described above, it is possible to develop more balanced and emotionally grounded strategies that may include elements of dismissing and preoccupied strategies. When a child develops in a context of care that is mostly warm, responsive, and predictable, they learn to rely on words and feelings to predict future events. When their requests for reassurance and comfort are heeded, they learn to trust others and this provides the context in which they learn to integrate their experiences and to give a good account of themselves, others and their relationships. They come to recognise that they are worthy and deserving of others' attention and they learn to respond empathically around others. The experience of "felt security" in adult close relationships has been summarised in the work of Mikulincer and Shaver (2007). Correlational research shows a positive relationship between self-reported felt security on the one hand, and less reactivity in affect regulation resulting in more support seeking, more open and curious information processing with a greater tolerance of uncertainty, more empathic, collaborative and assertive communication, and a more elaborated sense of self.

Bowlby (1973) observed we may respond with anger when we are faced with actual loss and rejection or the threat of loss, rejection, and abandonment. The expression of such anger in close relationships is thought to show a wish for connection, either in the anger of hope ("What do I have to do to get you to pay attention to me!!") or in the anger of despair ("You are a waste of space and I wish you'd never been born!!"). Both expressions may conceal feelings of sadness, shame, and fear that may be overlooked when others become organised by the anger and their own fear. Alcohol may well disinhibit the expression of anger for someone who relies on a deactivating or dismissing strategy of emotion regulation. Their expression of anger may be experienced as an intrusion, and come as a surprise to all. It is likely to be a source of shame for the person concerned especially if there is a family history of inhibiting anger because anger is feared as both dangerous and uncontrollable. On the other hand, the expression of anger in the context of hyper activating strategies can lead to exaggeration of both the anger and the concomitant vulnerability. Semantic explanations may be reduced in an attempt to manage the complexity and unpredictability of responding with anger, leading to the perpetuation of simplified beliefs about others. Strategies for processing negative affect and understanding the consequences on others may be underdeveloped, and alcohol use may reinforce these patterns.

Systemic therapy and attachment narratives: ANT

Rudi Dallos and I have been working for a number of years to integrate systems theory and practice with attachment theory and narrative theory. We believe this integration promotes a richer understanding and formulation of individual and relationship distress across all representational systems. This informs how we construct emotional and physical safety and promote resilient responding in our therapeutic practice. There are four aspects or domains of practice within an ANT approach: a) creating a secure base; b) exploring narratives and attachments within a systemic framework; c) considering alternatives—emotional risks and change; and d) the future—maintaining the therapeutic base. We have written extensively about these four domains elsewhere, but I shall summarise them here (Dallos & Vetere, 2009; Vetere & Dallos, 2008).

a. Creating a secure base in therapy involves containment, working towards emotional safety and promoting reflection on thought, action, emotion, and choice. The focus is on building support through the development of trust in the therapeutic relationship. Engagement and the therapeutic alliance are paramount, as is the case in all psychotherapies. Attachment theory emphasises the emotional processes of the secure base and the safe haven, for example, offering validation of experience, acknowledging the emotional risks and the demands of therapy, and the temptation to withdraw. We clarify the context of communication, for example, how we shall communicate. We work slowly, establishing a sense of safety with careful pacing and regular feedback. In relationship work we help to identify and explore unhelpful patterns of interaction, such that we might predict and prevent further distressing escalation.

b. The focus in the second domain is on exploration—identifying attachment dilemmas and ambivalence in people's relationships, such as attachment threats, attachment fears, attachment injuries, attachment longings, and divided loyalties. Such dilemmas can trigger further drinking or support a growing reliance on substance use if not processed and resolved. We help to identify and name attachment needs and wishes, for example, the need for comfort and reassurance and their underlying core patterns of thinking, feeling, and behaviour. We notice discrepancies and dysfluencies in how people talk about themselves and their relationships, for example, our head and heart. We explore problems, emotions, competencies, and success whilst promoting empathy, curiosity, and good listening. For someone to take the risk of accessing powerful emotional and relational experiences they need to know others will listen and not use the information against them in some way to hurt them. The work is slow and careful. When drinking is the issue, we advise the couple not to discuss sensitive topics unless they are sober and if it is not safe to revisit conflict at home in the early stages of our work, we encourage them to bring the issues for discussion to the therapy meetings.

c. The third domain of therapeutic practice is concerned with considering alternatives, promoting change and supporting relational and emotional risk taking. Acknowledging the risks of change and the threats to the perception of self and others begins to loosen the attachment dilemmas. As unhelpful patterns are both de-escalated and prevented, and there is more listening and reflection for people in their close relationships, they can both trust and own the changes. More satisfying and affirming communication, feeling good about each other, noticing and exchanging more positive moments, and seeking, giving and receiving comfort begin to consolidate the desired changes in relationships. Conflict resolution both inside and outside the home is addressed.

d. This final domain is concerned with the future and how we maintain the therapeutic base. We help family members develop shared narratives of how they healed their relationships and how they developed their preferred ways of being looked after. We acknowledge the possibility of "relapse" and a return to old patterns and habits of behaviour. We support the further development of communication and problem solving skills and identify what support they can both offer and draw upon in the future. Consolidation of desired changes involves creating opportunities for future reflection and holding each other in mind, that is, how we will think about each other and what we shall remember about each other in the future.

In conclusion, we believe that the integration of systems theory and practice with attachment theory and theory of narrative development both provides a platform for integrated, developmental formulations of the development of psychological problems in our close relationships and provides a map for how we help family members solve these problems creatively and kindly. Understanding and regulating our emotional experiences, giving and receiving comfort and care, and creating emotional safety for the development of narrative skills underpin well-being for individuals, families, and communities. Systemic theory gives us the tools to develop process based understandings of these powerful and significant human experiences and empathic appreciation of the dilemmas that affect us all.

References

Anderson, H., Goolishian, H., & Winderman, I. (1986). Problem-determined systems: toward transformation in family therapy. *Journal of Strategic and Family Therapy, 4*: 1–13.
Bowlby, J. (1973). *Attachment and Loss, Volumes 1 and 2*. New York: Basic Books.

Carter, B., & McGoldrick, M. (1988). *The Changing Family Life Cycle: Framework for Family Therapy* (2nd edition). New York: Gardner.

Crittenden, P. (2006). A dynamic-maturational model of attachmesnt. *Australian and New Zealand Journal of Family Therapy, 27*: 105–115.

Dallos, R., & Vetere, A. (2009). *Systemic Therapy and Attachment Narratives: Applications in a Range of Clinical Settings.* London: Routledge.

Mikulincer, M., & Shaver, P. (2007). *Attachment in Adulthood: Structure, Dynamics and Change.* New York: Guilford Press.

O'Farrell, T. J., & Fals-Stewart, W. (2002). Alcohol abuse. In: D. H. Sprenkle (Ed.), *Effectiveness Research in Marriage and Family Therapy* (pp. 123–162). Alexandria, V.A: American Association of Marriage and Family Therapy.

Reder, P., & Fredman, G. (1996). The relationship to help: Interacting beliefs about the treatment process. *Clinical Child Psychology and Psychiatry, 1*: 457–467.

Tulving, E. (1983). *Elements of Episodic Memory.* Oxford: Oxford University Press.

Vetere, A., & Dallos, R. (2008). Systemic therapy and attachment narratives. *Journal of Family Therapy, 30*: 374–385.

Vetere, A., & Henley, M. (2001). Integrating couples and family therapy into a community alcohol service: a pan-theoretical approach. *Journal of Family Therapy, 23*: 85–101.

CHAPTER FIVE

Taking the toys away: removing the need for self-harming behaviour

Lynn Greenwood

I first worked with Debbie when she was admitted to the in-patient eating-disorders unit of a private hospital for an eight-week treatment programme to address her entrenched patterns of food restriction, bingeing and vomiting. My weekly session of psychotherapy was part of a broader programme of psychological and practical groups, regular time with a key-worker and occasional appointments with a dietician; pretty standard in such an environment.

Debbie was thirty-one, married to Steve for five years and employed at the senior level of middle management by a blue-chip company. She was diagnosed with bulimia nervosa, symptoms of which include frequent episodes of binge eating and behaviours designed to compensate for this (laxatives, self induced vomiting, diuretics, over-exercise) plus a self-image that is defined by weight and body shape.

Debbie found her stay on the unit very difficult. The other patients were all severely underweight and on weight-gain diets (at least 0.6 kg per week) with the aim of reaching a BMI (Body Mass Index) of at least twenty.

The World Health Organization defines a healthy BMI as between 18.5 and twenty-five. However, this is global, including countries where food is scarce and people function at a lower weight. The use of

BMI as an indicator of healthy or unhealthy weight is not foolproof: for example, it doesn't differentiate between muscle and fat. Someone who does a lot of weight training may have low body-fat percentage but a BMI of over thirty: her muscularity not excess fat affects the measurement. In the UK, most eating disorder units aim for anorexic patients to achieve a BMI of at least twenty, gained by eating a "prescribed" diet and abstaining from exercise until the individual is well enough to be able to keep this within healthy limits.

Debbie's BMI was 31.5. However, her meal plan was designed to maintain her weight so that she wasn't left feeling physiologically and psychologically deprived. Like many people with bulimia, Debbie had embarked on endless crash diets that served only to drive her back to bingeing. It is important that patients who binge eat (or have a problem with significant overeating) first get their food under control, managing a regular and healthy meal plan for about two years before losing weight in a planned, gradual manner. This is to ensure that they aren't propelled back into the familiar binge starve cycle.

In her therapy sessions, Debbie often expressed her horror at eating alongside a "stick insect", perhaps with a BMI of less than sixteen, who had screamed that it was unfair she had to eat potatoes when she was getting so fat. Debbie wept: "How does she think I feel when she says something like that? It makes me feel so disgusting and greedy."

The main aim of Debbie's treatment was to regularise her eating, to provide her with coping mechanisms other than bingeing, vomiting, and restriction and to help her gain some insight into why she resorted to self-harming behaviour.

Debbie arrived for her first session with me with a brittle smile on her face and an amazing sense of humour with which she sought to camouflage her discomfort, anxiety, and unhappiness. During that appointment, she outlined her history.

Childhood

Her mother, Julia, was sixteen and in a new relationship when she fell pregnant. A "shotgun wedding" followed. The relationship was poor from the start; Debbie's father walked out when she was two. At that point, mum's weight plummeted and she and her daughter went to live with Julia's mother. Debbie remembered that it was her job to take food to her bed-ridden mother, earning extra praise from Nan if she managed to persuade Julia to eat. Dad cruised from woman to woman, fathering more children and making little effort to keep in contact with his eldest daughter. When she was about six, Debbie spotted him with a new "family"; he crossed the street, in her view, to avoid her. Decades followed with only sporadic contact with him; her paternal grand-mother "brokered" what little contact there was.

Debbie was convinced her dad avoided her only because there was something wrong with her. She was a disappointment, he was repulsed by her, or he thought she was boring. To compensate, she went out of her way to send him birthday and Christmas cards and presents that were never reciprocated.

By the time she was eight, Debbie was using food to comfort her-self and was already plump (although not, she later realised, "fat", the word her mother often threw at her in anger or disappointment). Julia remarried a wealthy man whose employer transferred him to the other side of the country. Debbie's memories of that time centred on watch-ing her increasingly emaciated mother as she toyed distractedly with a salad sandwich. She also lost regular contact with Nan, the closest thing she had to a "secure base" (Bowlby, 1988).

As soon as Debbie started school, Julia fiercely pushed her daughter academically, often demanding why a high mark wasn't even higher. Debbie told me that she'd been delighted to receive a merit for a violin exam, rushed home expecting praise, only to be asked, "Why didn't you get a distinction?" Alongside mum's concern with academic achieve-ment came constant criticism of Debbie's appearance (or, more accu-rately, weight).

Winnicott's (1960) theories of the development of the True and False Self highlight the impact of the events of Debbie's infancy. He writes:

> the good-enough mother meets the omnipotence of the infant and to some extent makes sense of it. She does this repeatedly. A True Self begins to have life, through the strength given to the infant's weak ego by the mother's implementation of the infant's omnipo-tent expressions.
>
> The mother who is not good enough is not able to implement the infant's omnipotence, and so she repeatedly fails to meet the infant gesture; instead she substitutes her own gesture which is to be given sense by the compliance of the infant. This compliance on the part of the infant is the earliest stage of the False Self, and belongs

to the mother's inability to sense her infant's needs. (Winnicott, 1960, p. 145)

From a very early age, Debbie's role was to meet her mother's needs. With Nan's well intentioned encouragement, Debbie had focused her efforts on easing her mother's distress, a pattern that soon became entrenched. Winnicott (1960) describes the consequences of such a situation:

> [W]here the mother cannot adapt well enough, the infant gets seduced into a compliance, and a compliant False Self reacts to environmental demands and the infant seems to accept them. Through this False Self the infant builds up a false set of relationships, and by means of introjections even attains a show of being real, so that the child may grow to be just like mother, nurse, aunt, brother, or whoever at the time dominates the scene. The False Self has one positive and very important function: to hide the True Self, which it does by compliance with environmental demands. (Winnicott, 1960, p. 146)

Debbie received a very particular demand from her environment. Mother had issues with food: at that time, anorexia, a condition in which the sense of self is inextricably linked to size, weight, and appearance. People with anorexia often feel that it is only by restricting food to a sometimes dangerous level that they can communicate their fragility and vulnerability. Maintaining a low weight, or even continuing to drop kilos, gives an illusion of control. Anorexia has similarities to drink or drug addiction in that it takes the edge off difficult feelings and becomes the route through which all emotion is expressed.

Just as it isn't possible to conduct therapy with someone who's drunk or high on cocaine, therapy with someone whose weight is dangerously low is likely to engage only with "anorexia": cognition and communication may be seriously compromised. (That said, when working on an adolescent unit, I've spent time at the bedside of a young person, hoping that talking gently to her, without any expectation of a response, may start to establish a therapeutic alliance on which we can build as her weight gradually increases. Unfortunately, resources are now so limited that they tend to be focused on those patients deemed able to use psychotherapy in a more conventional way.)

Debbie's mother was a child-woman who, because of her own undiagnosed problems (originating in a disturbed childhood and exacerbated by her brief, unsuccessful marriage), was only able to think about herself, her diet, and her appearance. She looked to her daughter to fulfil her own unrealised ambitions, expressing disappointment if Debbie didn't come top of the class ("What grades did the others get?") and relentlessly criticising her appearance.

So many times, I have worked with women and girls (and some men) with eating disorders whose mothers also have issues with food and body image. At its most simple, the problem can be in a mother's quest for the "perfect" body (in truth, a self that has no flaws or vulnerability), continually embarking on diets and detoxes in the hope of shedding a few pounds, or, perhaps more accurately, ridding herself of the bottom, thighs or stomach that she regards as "fat" but are actually well within the realms of "healthy". Watching mum cut out carbohydrates and serve herself smaller portions than the rest of the family can have a serious impact on a child. Overruling hunger and denying one's self becomes seen almost as a badge of honour. Similarly, the daughter starts to feel repulsed by her mother's body and ultimately by her own.

Just as mother hates every part of her body that doesn't comply with rules dictated by air-brushed pictures in fashion magazines, the daughter sees her own body as imperfect. The more her own body shape resembles that of her mother, the greater her self-disgust, particularly if mum is severely overweight.

At the other extreme is the "yummy mummy" who spends hours trying to make herself look "perfect": exercise, an overly rigid diet, visits to beauty salons, surgical "procedures" (non-invasive and otherwise), clothes that might be the wrong side of "too young". She believes that she isn't acceptable unless she looks flawless and, consciously or unconsciously, ends up competing with a teenaged daughter who may be gawky, covered in acne and struggling with developing breasts. I've seen young women enter into an uncompromising battle with their own body that they can't win without feeling that they've also destroyed their mother, which may be an unconscious expression of rage. The body becomes something almost to be beaten into submission. I've also worked with those who remove themselves from the competition not only by binge or overeating but treating their body and appearance with total disregard and disgust.

With her own difficult history, an unplanned pregnancy and a relationship that was probably unstable from the start, Julia was ill equipped to be an effective mother. When her husband left she fell into a depression. André Green's theory of the "Dead Mother Complex" explores the impact on an infant of a depressed parent, unable to respond to her child and effectively dissociating from, or even killing off, her own inner life. He points out that as a result of maternal depression:

> Independently of the spontaneous evolution towards the depressive position, there has been an important maternal contribution which intervenes, disturbing the positive outcome of the depressive phase and complicating the conflict, because of the reality of maternal decathexis which is sufficiently perceptible by the infant, to wound his narcissism. (Green, 1986, p. 169)

Gianna Williams' (1977) view of anorexia as a "no-entry" system of defences, highlights further the emotional unavailability of Debbie's mother. She describes anorexia as a condition that prevents intrusion or "trespass". Indeed, there is something powerful about the denial of appetite and the literal and symbolic refusal to ingest. Williams concludes her paper with a paragraph that emphasises the legacy that Julia passed on to her daughter:

> Bion (1959, pp. 308–315) spoke of "nameless dread" when he was talking of the return of projections which have not been received, contained, metabolised, by the parental object … However, I would like to suggest that the definition of nameless dread applies just as much to, and is the most appropriate definition I have found up to now for, the experience of a child when he or she is used as a receptacle of parental projections. (Williams, 1997, p. 122)

From an early age, Debbie saw her role as achieving and pleasing a mother who appeared unable to accept her daughter for who she was. Similarly, Debbie found herself trapped in a cycle of trying, through unacknowledged gifts and cards, to placate a father whom she was convinced she'd disappointed. Unsurprisingly, by the time she reached adolescence, food had become a main source of comfort.

Adolescence and sexuality

The family returned to their home town when Debbie was about eleven, shortly after she'd started secondary education at boarding school. She continued to board for three or four years. At the end of term, when she was about fourteen, she returned home to find only her stepfather at home. He told her that, some weeks earlier, Julia had left him and moved back with her own mother. She was so consumed by her own pain that she hadn't even considered breaking this news to her daughter. Debbie appeared to have accepted philosophically the loss of another father figure. She eventually moved into a new home with her mother, changed schools and rarely spoke to me about this man; perhaps because she was forced to attend to her mother rather than any feelings she might have had about Julia's second unsuccessful marriage.

By now, Debbie's mother was over-eating, rather than under-eating. (It isn't uncommon for anorexia to shift into bulimia: food is the common factor in both conditions.) She ballooned. The larger Julia grew, the more she attacked her daughter's size. She became caught on the binge–starve merry-go-round, each time believing that she'd eventually manage to lose weight and not regain it. Debbie's eating now also became more out of control, binges worsened, alternately curtailed and then fuelled by extreme dieting.

Adulthood

Julia was determined that her daughter was going to study architecture at university. However, for the first time in her life, Debbie rebelled. Even with extremely strong A-level grades, she found a fairly menial job as an assistant in the haberdashery department of the local branch of a major retailer.

Around the same time, Julia started dating Keith. Within a few months she was living with him, leaving Debbie to live alone in (and pay the rent on) the flat they'd previously shared. Debbie visited her mum and her new partner frequently. For a while, Julia's weight remained stable, perhaps because of the pressure she felt by Keith's "interest" in provocative photographs of naked or near-naked women.

Debbie had only learned about sex at school. Her mother had left a book on her bed in her early teens but said nothing directly. In fact, Debbie once told me that the only discussion she ever had with Julia was when her mother told her that "it's very over-rated". This coupled, with the revulsion with her own body that Julia had projected into her, made her vulnerable to sexual exploitation and abuse.

A few months into her job, Debbie became the target for her much older manager, George. He'd engineer it so that he was often alone with her in the stock room. What started with inappropriate sexual comments escalated to him forcing her to perform oral sex. Debbie was scared and overly compliant, particularly because George insisted that his attentions were "her fault". The situation escalated. On Debbie's days off, he would know she was at home and often drop round to her flat. She told no one and never felt safe. This went on for a year or more until George was transferred to another branch. Many years later and some way into her therapy, Debbie heard that someone had complained about George, who was sacked and charged with a sexual offence. However, for her, the shame belonged not to her abuser but to her.

It was at this point that Debbie started to make herself sick. Originally associated with the disgust she felt after an unwanted sexual act, self-induced vomiting became important symbolically in ridding herself of the food on which she'd gorged herself, something she initially regarded as soothing and "good" but which soon turned "bad" and had to be expelled.

Friday night was pub night for Debbie and her colleagues. She felt ill at ease at these events and drank heavily. She became the target for another colleague, Jonathan, who enjoyed sadistic sex, often biting and beating her. Again, Debbie felt she had no option but to comply, hiding her bites and bruises with high necklines or scarves. After about a year, the abuse stopped when Jonathan left the company. By this time, alcohol and vomiting had become part of Debbie's painful "portfolio" of self-harming behaviours.

One Friday night in the pub, Debbie was approached by a stranger. She never discovered his name but accompanied him back to his flat, in her words, "a stinking hovel". He raped her anally. Debbie managed to leave and get home. From this point, her self-harming behaviour worsened.

Despite these traumatic events, she flourished at work and was promoted regularly. However, part of this was down to an obsessive fear of getting things wrong, checking and rechecking documents countless times and working well over ten hours a day and at weekends.

Shortly afterwards, Debbie met and married Steve, a friend of a friend's husband. Steve was a timid and not particularly ambitious man. Even though he was eight years older than she was, Debbie soon outstripped him at work. She earned far more than he did and was promoted to head office.

They had been married about a year when things spiralled out of control and she finally agreed to be admitted to hospital. It isn't uncommon for symptoms to escalate once someone is out of a toxic environment, almost as though the decreased need to protect against intrusions or attacks creates a different kind of vulnerability.

Early stages of treatment

What emerged during Debbie's eight-week admission, when we first worked together, was a young woman in a totally enmeshed relationship with her mother and preoccupied by her father's abandonment of her mother (and the expectation that her husband would do the same). She hated talking about Julia in any way that could be seen as critical. I suggested that there were three of us in the room: Debbie, me, and Julia. She didn't disagree and would throw anxious glances at the empty sofa alongside her chair.

Even though both she and Julia were in long-term, committed relationships, she spoke as if she and her mother were the couple, more than that, she perceived herself to be totally responsible for her mother's wellbeing. She explained that she and Steve had chosen to live west of London, partly because they worked in central London but didn't want to live centrally and partly because her aim was to move as far from Julia's demands as possible. Yet it wasn't unusual for Debbie to drop everything after a phone call because Julia had sounded anxious and depressed and she was convinced it was her job to drive 300 miles to '"fix" her. Julia only visited her daughter once while she was in hospital. According to Debbie, she drank tea and chatted as though she'd dropped in on a weekend break in a luxury hotel, not once did she ask about her daughter's condition or treatment.

In the strict containment of the eating disorders unit, Debbie's bingeing and vomiting were brought under control and she was eating healthy, balanced, regular meals. However, she was desperate to "escape", as she put it, and pressured her consultant psychiatrist to discharge her. He did. She was to continue following her meal plan and see both me and her key-worker once a week and her consultant every six weeks. Her key-worker helped Debbie think through a phased return to work so that she could resume responsibilities gradually rather than risk feeling she taken on too much too soon.

This plan fell apart pretty quickly. Within a few weeks, Debbie was working full time, although she was scrupulous about keeping her appointments with me. (That said, I wondered with her whether this was as much down to her sense that I was the mother with particular expectations as to her believing that what we were doing was important to her.) She became more anxious and chaotic. Her meal plan had turned into a diet: Debbie started shedding kilos, dropping from 100 kg to around eighty-five kg within three months of being discharged.

While she started wearing more colourful clothes, and told me that she was following my example of wearing coordinated jewellery, her anxiety about her appearance was through the roof, fed partly by Julia's constant messages that Debbie looked much better in black and she really shouldn't wear her hair that long. Coupled with this was the belief that she was living on borrowed time at work, her managers had been overly generous in allowing her to take so much time off and now they were only waiting for an opportunity to sack her. Debbie's obsession with checking became even worse than it had been prior to her admission to hospital. She was also convinced that Steve was on the brink of leaving her, terrified that if she were away from home on a business trip, another woman would be in bed with him.

It was only now that Debbie admitted to the full catalogue of self-harming behaviours:

- bingeing
- vomiting
- food restriction
- smoking
- overwork
- laxative abuse
- over-exercise
- alcohol abuse
- self-harm (cutting and burning)
- abusing caffeinated drinks (twelve cans of Diet Coke a day)
- abusing caffeine tablets.

What emerged was that Debbie had been too ashamed to disclose the full list of self-harming behaviours on her first admission. More than that, she was terrified at the thought of giving up the only thing that she knew would calm her overwhelming feelings of anxiety, terror, and self-hatred.

Debbie also told me that she would encourage Steve to perpetrate the same sexual acts that she'd been forced to perform by George, Jonathan, and the person she called "The Man with No Name". Sex was generally followed by some form of self-harm that Debbie hoped would numb the feelings of fear, disgust, and shame. Obsessive Compulsive Disorder (OCD) was another problem she finally had the courage to tell me about. Debbie kept antibacterial gel or wipes in virtually every room of the house, in the car and at work; she bought eight bottles of bleach a week and wouldn't eat food unless there were even numbers. She carefully counted potatoes and even peas; such things as spaghetti and rice were a total no-no.

The first four symptoms were in the assessment conducted before her admission. She had been too terrified and ashamed to disclose the other six or her OCD.

Following her discharge and with bingeing, vomiting, and restriction more or less under control, Debbie started to turn to other self-harming behaviours in a desperate effort to sooth her terrors not uncommon and something that make this so-called "multi-impulsivity" so difficult to treat (Lacey & Evans, 1986); particularly now that financial constraints have further limited the ability of the NHS to provide effective containment (even adequate treatment in a private hospital depends on "deep pockets" or an unusually generous medical insurance policy).

Eventually, Debbie was spending two or three hours a day in the loo at work, bingeing on packets of chocolate muffins and then making herself sick. Nothing I could offer appeared to her to be as effective as her own "solutions". Just as Julia had communicated to Debbie that she was useless, Debbie was now giving me a similar message.

We went from one to two to three sessions per week (by now, in my private practice). While Debbie insisted that she wanted to stop harming herself, she couldn't or wouldn't allow any space between a difficult feeling that might spiral out of control and bingeing or cutting or taking laxatives or whatever she imagined might be most effective at the time. She described how Steve had started following her around the house, trying to ensure that she wasn't about to cut or to burn herself "accidentally on purpose" while she was ironing. Debbie resented this intrusion and tried to explain to him that if she was intent on self-harming, there was nothing he could do about it. I suggested to her that she was delivering a similar message to me.

Not only was Debbie launching a horrendous attack on her body, she was also attacking her therapy, nothing I could offer quite "hit the spot" (as she put it) in the same way as hurting herself. In the absence of a caring mother to soothe her fears and anxiety, Debbie had turned to damaging her own despised, (by herself and by Julia), body to try and cope with what life threw at her. Even though the experience of release or numbness is temporary, Debbie had some confidence they worked.

While addressing lapses and even minor relapses is grist to the mill in psychotherapy with patients who attack their bodies, there is a point at which continuing the work can be a collusion. Debbie was showing me almost triumphantly that whatever I had to offer, she preferred to hurt herself. Working with individuals with anorexia, a similar situation is often presented either by a relentless loss of kilos or the maintenance of an unhealthily low weight. A frequent anorexic fantasy is to "have it all", to lead a rich and fulfilling life and to remain emaciated. In my work with South West London & St. George's Eating Disorders Service, we often thought about patients being "ready" to face the challenge of giving up their self-damaging behaviours. Sometimes it takes two or three treatments for someone to be able to find the trust in the team, the determination and inner resources to continue working on a programme towards recovery. Sadly many people are unable to take even the first few steps. Those who are critically underweight often have countless stabilisation admissions, designed largely to do no more than keep them alive.

Recognising Debbie's attack on her therapy, I challenged her, saying that she was using her sessions only to list the ways in which she was hurting herself. We explored how this was both an expression of desperation and of contempt, in the transference, I was another mother who was ill equipped to support her. I said that, with this in mind, she should consider whether it was the right time to stop her self-harming behaviour or whether it was time to work towards an ending. Her consultant psychiatrist delivered a similar message. Debbie decided on a second admission; this time she was treated on a general ward rather than the eating disorders unit. I saw her twice a week, once again as part of her treatment programme.

Debbie found life on the general ward even more difficult than the eight weeks she'd spent on the eating disorders unit. She was desperate to leave but also recognised that discharging herself prematurely would make it even more likely that she would unravel and end up in treatment yet again. She was also concerned that she'd lose both her job and her husband.

Her second admission lasted twelve weeks. While her return to work was gradual, Debbie admitted "cheating" by putting in additional hours at home. It would be wonderful to be able to say that she had been "cured" of the impulse to hurt herself. With close observation by and the support of professionals, Debbie had started to manage the urges to self-harm. She also learned that rushes of anxiety ebbed rather than continuing on an inexorable, excruciating exponential curve. However, on leaving hospital, she again faced the challenge of dealing with pressures of day-to-day life without her familiar "coping mechanisms".

Psychotherapeutic work

On Debbie's second discharge from hospital, we returned to three sessions a week in an attempt to contain stress and anxiety and the consequent urge to self-harm. Whether she was seeing me on hospital premises or in my private practice, she was scrupulous about respecting the frame, rarely missing a session, arriving on the dot and paying promptly. However, this, we considered, was as much about her believing that I was seeing her on sufferance and was likely to abandon her. On more than one occasion, she said: "I'm so frightened that I'm going to ring the bell and you're not going to be here." She found it puzzling that I'd willingly spend three hours a week with her, particularly as, in her view, her body was smelly and disgusting, the legacy of the sexual abuse she'd experienced.

Whenever I tried to explore the transference, she'd curtail the subject as fast as she could: "Oh, no. Not this again. I told you. You don't have a life outside here: you live in the filing cabinet in the corridor". Even when I challenged her that she'd once seen me in the street, she flatly refused to put her feelings or fantasies into words: "Well, I suppose you need to get some exercise from time to time. It's probably quite cramped in there".

I suspect that Debbie was defending against my needs becoming more important than hers, if she started to acknowledge that I had an existence beyond the consulting room, I might become the mother who sought to use her only to meet her own needs. As long as she could convince herself that I had no needs (I was a part object), I wasn't a threat. I never found out whether this hunch was accurate, she resolutely refused to engage with me on the matter. Similarly, she could pretend if I didn't exist, there was no real relationship—or possibility of abandonment by me.

Containing self-harming behaviours

Even after her second admission, Debbie found it impossible to refrain from hurting herself if she felt under pressure. While lapses (or relapses) were often intense and alarming, this time, I had a sense that she was risking putting more energy into trying not to use self-harming behaviours.

In working with patients who self-harm, I spend some time looking at distraction techniques or coping mechanisms. It isn't easy for someone to avoid the "lure" of cutting, with its immediate sense of release or numbing, and choose instead to phone a friend or play loud music or focus on solving a Sudoku puzzle or watch *West Side Story* for the umpteenth time. Again and again, Debbie dutifully made lists of things she could do instead of bingeing, purging, or taking caffeine tablets. More than once, she arrived at her session and admitted that she was carrying laxatives or razor blades. She always left them behind with me and I began to have a little more confidence that in confiding in me, she was signalling that we had an alliance and she wanted both to use me as a container for her unbearable emotions and accept my help.

While she was getting strong signals that she was highly valued at work, Debbie almost stubbornly refused to believe the evidence. Nearly every week, she reported the worry that she'd "done something wrong" and had spent hours either at home alone or at work in the disabled toilet bingeing and vomiting and ultimately putting herself under further pressure. I reflected that she was showing me her reluctance to give up using food to "stuff down" her difficult feelings. She exploded, "You're trying to take away my toys. There's nothing more wonderful than being alone, with the door shut and a bag full of chocolate. Anyway, when I've got my 'fuck-it' head on, there's nothing you or anybody else can do about it."

It was unrealistic to expect that in times of stress Debbie would magically move from hurting herself to the healthy coping techniques she'd learned in hospital and with me. While she could deal with some pressures during her session, she wasn't strong enough to manage a fragile and demanding mother, a sometimes difficult working environment and her relationship with a husband who was finding himself increasingly unable to cope with her self-harm. Furthermore, there is a stark reality: crises (real or perceived) don't organise themselves around my working hours. While weekends and breaks were particularly problematic, Debbie could leave my consulting room and within the hour find herself in a situation she experienced as overwhelming. It was through my work with her that I developed a new approach to my work with people who harm themselves (Greenwood, 2009).

I suggested that if she felt there was a high risk of self-harm, she could leave a message on my voicemail. This was subject to certain boundaries:

- I wasn't promising to return her calls. I'd contact her if I were able (or, in truth, wanted to)
- any phone conversation between us would last no more than ten minutes
- our focus would be on practicalities to prevent bingeing, vomiting, or other forms of self-harm. This would not be a mini therapy session.

This underlined the importance of our attachment relationship—and the fact that this involved necessary boundaries. Debbie rarely called. She didn't want to intrude and risk rejection. However, from time to time, I'd find a message saying that she was in her spare room to try and stop herself bingeing on a bagful of food she'd bought specially. It generally took a few minutes to work out with her how best to get rid of it (perhaps stamping on it and then driving a few miles to dump the bag in a bin). This was a turning point.

As her psychotherapy progressed, it wasn't unusual for me to pick up long voicemails describing a horrible situation and the feelings it evoked but ending with the words: "Ooooh, that's better. No need to call me back. I'll see you on Wednesday". My voicemail had become some kind of containing transitional object for her. The temporary soothing qualities of her "toys" were gradually fading.

Debbie was the first person with whom I worked in this way. There have been a number of others. Only once has a patient left messages whenever she felt the stirrings of anxiety rather than when she was at risk of using behaviours, an issue we addressed in her sessions.

About three years into our work together, Debbie managed to stop cutting and burning. It was a gradual process rather than a sudden stop. However, she started drinking more heavily, often in secret, at home. Gradually, she brought this under control. One by one, over a period of years rather than weeks or months, she stopped virtually all her behaviours. Debbie would paint her nails rather than cut, after all, you can't wield a knife or razor blade effectively if your varnish is tacky. She'd ring a friend instead of drinking or go for a bike ride instead of taking laxatives.

Her husband, in truth dependent on Debbie and not without problems of his own, found it hard to stop himself checking what she was doing when she was at home and out of his sight. She found this infuriating: "Steve keeps following me around to make sure I haven't got food or a knife. I've told him and I'm telling you, just in case there's any doubt, I'm never going back to 'That Place' (the hospital) again". In fact, Steve saw a therapist for about a year to explore his own unresolved issues around loss and to help him recognise that his wife had to want to stop hurting herself, he could be supportive but the final decision was ultimately hers.

Slowly, Debbie was even able to challenge her OCD, the eight bottles of bleach per week went down to an occasional purchase. When we first started to explore her experience of abuse, her sense of herself as filthy and smelly increased dramatically and then ebbed. The only bottle of antibacterial gel that remained was by the kitchen sink.

The one thing that was difficult for her to get totally under control was food. While she stopped bingeing, Debbie struggled not to overeat. Even though she occasionally returned to her recommended meal plan, she increased to her highest ever weight. At one point, we agreed that I'd weigh her weekly. She'd slowly and erratically drift down from 115 kg towards 110 kg but then shoot upwards again. The weekly weighing had become a counterproductive and humiliating experience, she was starting to see me as a punitive superego (her mother). We decided that weighing, or not, would be something for which she would take responsibility.

Relationships

Debbie's relationships with her parents were a key focus for most of her therapy. "There must be something wrong with me, otherwise Dad would keep in touch." "I have to look after my mother". We worked together for eight years. During all that time, she only saw her father once, at her grandfather's funeral. His mother, whom she visited increasingly rarely, kept her up-to-date with his news. Slowly, she moved from seeing herself as the flawed child and began to reassess him. "This is the third relationship he's had with someone younger than me. Pillock". "I never told you about my dad's tattoos. Granny says that he's almost covered with them. And she told me he's covered in fake tan. What an arsehole". (At times, Debbie's language was ripe and became increasingly so as she stopped self-harming.)

One year, he wrote to her at Christmas bemoaning the way his life had turned out and the terrible hand he'd been dealt. "Like he's such a victim. Poor thing". Finally, Debbie was able to express her rage towards him and more than a little contempt. She stopped sending presents and cards.

Her relationship with her mother was trickier. In the early stages of therapy, Debbie told me that she and her husband visited Julia and her partner at least once a month. She found these visits intolerable. However often she explained that discussing food and weight was triggering for her, Julia would insist on venting her own anxieties. If they went out to dinner, her mother would start fretting about the number of calories on her plate. One month, she'd crow that she'd lost four or five kilos through a crash diet. The next month, she'd become tearful because she'd put it all back on again, plus more.

Debbie felt that she had a responsibility towards Julia and her husband (both of them hugely overweight). She was earning a generous salary and often paid for them to join her and Steve on holiday. She would treat them to meals out, Julia constantly craved calorie-laden food but would then start crying about her weight and appearance. She still criticised Debbie for disobeying her edicts to dress in black and keep her hair short.

Very slowly, Debbie stopped reacting defensively if I suggested that she may have found Julia's behaviour unkind, upsetting, or infuriating. First, she stopped phoning her every night; then, she and Steve reduced their monthly visits, occasionally opting to stay in a hotel rather than under Julia's roof. Instead of regular holidays together, Debbie paid for Julia and her partner to go away on their own. The second time this happened, Julia rang her daughter from Stockholm to complain about the hotel. Debbie was furious: "She said she didn't want me to be upset but she needed to let me know that it had been a waste of my money. She told me that the room was dirty and the bed uncomfortable. She suggested that I write and complain".

Julia could feel her daughter finally separating from her and becoming more circumspect about what she disclosed to her. Debbie recognised her mother's ranting phone call from Sweden as a retaliatory attack. Not only was she threatened by her daughter's individuation, she was also envious of her relationship with me. She'd ask regularly: "Are you still seeing Thingummybob?" Debbie mused with a barely concealed delight, "Jesus, Lynn, you've got the same name as her sister. As if she'd forget that!"

What became apparent was that as Debbie took increasingly large steps towards a healthy lifestyle, her mother's mental health unravelled. Her weight spiralled totally out of control. Her anxiety was through the roof, to the point that she rarely left home. Debbie tried to encourage her to go to the GP, only to receive the cutting response: "I'm not like you. I don't need pills and I don't need therapy".

As Debbie stopped containing her mother's anxiety, stress, and pressure, Julia's psychological state deteriorated. By now, though, Debbie was less affected by guilt or emotional blackmail and more aware of the role her mother had played in her own condition.

A parallel situation with her husband emerged. Debbie became more confident, better able to socialise and more assertive at work. She was promoted two or three times in a fairly short space of time. Steve had never been ambitious or a high-flyer; even when she was at her most ill, Debbie had earned more than he did and assumed more than half of the responsibility for joint decisions. Debbie talked of arguments about whether DVDs should be arranged alphabetically by title or alphabetically by title within genres and her frustration with Steve's endless lists. In truth, he too had OCD traits and was totally dependent on his wife. She recounted how she'd been packing for a two-night business trip and found him crying in the bathroom, so anxious was he about being left alone, or, perhaps, whom she might meet while he was away. It seemed that, in some ways, Debbie and Steve's respective pathologies "matched", both were terrified of abandonment.

It was clear from the start that Debbie's mother had projected all her distress, anxiety, and expectations into her daughter. What had been less clear was that this was also happening with Steve, who could camouflage his own insecurities and need behind the façade of a husband who was worried about an unstable wife.

Trauma work

Memories of abuse were often in Debbie's mind. Not only was her body central to her maladaptive coping mechanisms, it was almost like a prison from which she couldn't escape. First, years of critical comments by Julia had left their mark. Debbie had never been comfortable in her own skin, seeing herself as fat and ugly. Her mother's injunctions to hide herself in black hit the mark. On top of that were her memories of men using her body and her belief that she had no right to say "no".

A crowded lift, being jostled in the street, a hot day, everyday situations could trigger flashbacks of being hit, strangled, or raped. These were often accompanied by an overpowering recollection of smells; urine, drink, faeces, semen. She was terrified that her own vaginal secretions stank. Debbie described how she'd sometimes get off a train before her stop. In a packed carriage, she was worried equally that someone would sexually assault her or that people would be disgusted by her smell.

Disclosing the abuse was slow work. At times, particularly difficult sessions sparked episodes of self-harm or an increase in Debbie's OCD. It was impossible to think about the trauma without also addressing the punishment, either through self-harm or OCD, that she meted out on her body.

Unsurprisingly, she had stopped having sex with Steve shortly before her first hospital admission. When she told me that she had coerced him into acting out what her perpetrators had done, I suggested that she was scared he'd turn from a loving husband into rapist and wanted to retain an illusion of control. She leapt on this, "If I hadn't suggested it, he would have done. Only that way I wouldn't know what was coming: when it would hurt; where it would hurt. That's what always happens. You get hurt, one way or another."

It became apparent quite quickly that Debbie didn't really understand sex or how her body worked, things she thought were revolting were perfectly normal. She also had great difficulty using, hearing, or reading words for parts of the human anatomy or sexual acts. Once, when I said the word "penis", she leapt from her chair, shouting: "Yes, one of those." That was supposed to be my cue to shut up. However, we both persevered. Debbie ordered books online (she wouldn't consider browsing the shelves of a shop) and started the gruelling process of getting past the contents page. She decided instead to leaf through the index, only to encounter the same difficulty: "They're all dirty words. I don't know how people can write them, let alone say them".

We thought about how Debbie could become more accustomed to her body being touched. She started having regular manicures, then allowed Steve to moisturise her hands every evening. They booked weekend spa breaks, where Debbie would have massages, she was even more worried about the masseuse being disgusted by her than about being touched inappropriately. Eventually, she allowed Steve to massage her back. Then they started having baths together. I suddenly realised that she was no longer talking about the abuse. It was as if memories of those experiences had faded, to be replaced first by horror over the "obscene" words in the books Debbie was reading and then by the fear of an intimate relationship with her husband.

Moving on to kissing and caressing was more difficult. She became frightened if she could feel Steve becoming aroused. Months followed during which her therapy sessions were filled with fear and anxiety, not to mention her guilt that she was letting Steve down. He seemed endlessly patient and it occurred to me that sex might not be as high on his agenda as Debbie imagined it to be. I reflected with her that a lot of couples have celibate relationships. She didn't respond.

A few weeks later, she announced triumphantly: "We did it". She then explained: "It was my 'fuck-it head', I just got fed up with pulling back or telling Steve to stop or waiting to get frightened".

Ending

About three years before she formally ended therapy, Debbie was relocated to an office near Bristol. She worked longer hours than Steve, so the couple decided to move closer to her workplace. The train journey to London was over two hours. We decided that it was impracticable for her to continue coming to see me three times a week. She was anxious about this but we agreed that we could schedule an additional session by phone if things were tricky for her.

For the first year of this arrangement, Debbie attended virtually every session. If she had to go to a meeting, we'd speak on the phone. By this stage, her self-harming behaviours were much reduced and we never had to schedule an additional telephone appointment.

After a year in her new role, she was promoted. Gradually, the number of missed sessions increased, while her ability to keep even an appointment by phone decreased. Eventually, I pointed out to Debbie that about half of my monthly fee comprised of appointments she hadn't attended. We went down to one session a week. She still cancelled about half.

A few months later, Debbie was headhunted for a position in London. She reassured me that her attendance would be regular once she moved. It wasn't. She then explained that she just needed time to settle, her role was very senior and there was a lot to do.

Eight months later, I put it to her that her missed sessions were an unconscious communication that she wanted to stop therapy. She stared at me, clearly shaken. However, at the next session, she admitted that I was right.

Bowlby (1998) writes that

> the human infant comes into the world genetically biased to develop a set of behavioural patterns that, given an appropriate environment, will result in his keeping more or less close proximity to whomever cares for him, and that this tendency to maintain proximity serves the function of protecting the mobile infant and growing child from a number of dangers of predation is likely to have been paramount. (Bowlby, 1998, p. 68)

He goes on to say "it is the therapist's main role to provide her patient with a secure base" (Bowlby, 1998, p. 68).

It occurred to me that Debbie was using me as a secure base from which she was revisiting the world that she'd originally found herself ill-equipped to enter. As she felt more confident and better able to look after herself, she extended the periods of absence between us.

Debbie assured me that she wanted to end "properly" (her word), so we fixed an end date three months ahead just before the Easter break. Debbie promised she'd prioritise her sessions, my scepticism was justified.

Despite this, Debbie focused on looking back over her eight years in therapy. She felt that she had finally separated from her mother. She no longer felt responsible for Julia's wellbeing (even though her mother was clearly psychologically ill). While Julia still couldn't stop commenting on food, weight, and appearance, Debbie was better able to ignore these comments and not allow them to trigger her own spiral into self-disgust.

Her attitude towards her father had also changed significantly. She was no longer desperate to please him in the hope that he might pay her attention. Instead, she admitted that she'd written an angry letter to him. She hadn't sent it by the time we finished but I had the feeling that eventually she might.

Debbie had managed to stop virtually all her self-harming behaviours, even smoking. While still far above a healthy weight, Debbie was starting to control her overeating, chipping slowly away at the kilos, rather than resorting to the crazy crash diets she had once favoured. Overeating had been the first of her maladaptive coping mechanisms, so it was not surprising that it was the one she found most difficult to address. This is not uncommon, people relinquish last their "original" form of self-harm.

By now, she was also having a full sexual relationship with Steve. Looking back, she told me that she was stunned that she'd been celibate for over five years.

Debbie was now confident and assertive at work. She'd eventually realised that her managers weren't employing her out of pity but because she was highly efficient and effective. In starting her new job, she had encountered more than one aggressive colleague. Initially, she was anxious and perturbed but then discovered that she was more than able to stand her ground: "The truth is I don't care that much. What are they going to do? Fire me?"

There was one area that she still found hard: close friendships. In difficult times, her friends turned to her. Debbie found it impossible to confide in them. She was worried about being a burden but also that they wouldn't be able to cope with what she might want to discuss. I helped her see that this might have more to do with her choosing vulnerable, dependent friends rather than the awfulness of what she might disclose to them. While she didn't "drop" anyone, she started making it a priority to have lunch or dinner with former or current colleagues.

Her final session felt sad and awkward. Debbie didn't know what to say, she filled fifty minutes with halting reflections, even admitting that she found it all rather embarrassing. She left without saying either thank you or goodbye. Perhaps she was communicating that she wanted the option of coming back I felt almost disappointed, overlooked and abandoned, emotions with which I'm sure Debbie was all too familiar. Maybe I wanted warmth and appreciation from her; perhaps those were also the very qualities that neither of us was able to express in that final session.

Final thoughts

I would love to be able to say that Debbie's gradual relinquishment of her self-harming behaviours and move towards a healthier, fulfilling life are frequent outcomes. They aren't. I have known people, either seeing me privately or in a specialist unit, make a tremendous amount of progress before something triggers a calamitous return to square one. Sometimes it has to be acknowledged that "now isn't the right time" or while there may have been a little progress, the patient has come as far as she can. While it's important not to abandon someone while she's struggling, there's a fine line between support and collusion. It isn't easy to decide whether a patient is going through a rough patch or attacking therapy by a terrified refusal to stop harming herself. However, I believe that sometimes it's iatrogenic to continue working together unless there is at least some indication, through actions or attitude, of a gradual movement towards health.

With Debbie, there were periods, even after her second admission, when I wondered whether she had the capacity to give up her dangerous coping mechanisms. I once said to her that this might be all she could manage. Looking back, I suspect that this comment served to make her determined to continue towards a healthier lifestyle; she was highly competitive and hated a suggestion that something was beyond her.

Before I started working on this case study, I emailed Debbie asking permission to write about her, reassuring her that I would change all identifiable names and facts. She replied: "Please don't make me be from Manchester and I'd prefer not to be named after seasons or alcoholic beverages. I really appreciate all the help and support you gave me and am still often surprised by how robust I am now, so if agreeing to this is helpful to you then so much the better." I suspect it felt too difficult, maybe too intimate, to thank me face-to-face during our last session. Inadvertently, I'd offered her the perfect opportunity.

Working with Debbie underlined the importance of consistency and availability to someone who has been used to contain parental projections and anxieties. What use was I if I wasn't around at least occasionally when she was at her most desperate? Support by phone, I believe, proved to her that I took her seriously and although not reachable round the clock, I wasn't going to abandon her when she was at her most vulnerable. In time, she was able to use the phone symbolically: hearing (and being reassured by) my voicemail message, evacuating her distress into what she called a "rant" and finding this calming. I would listen to her message and know that she'd been distressed enough to want to self-harm but I'd know that on this occasion, she was alright without me. My voicemail was, for a time, a powerful transitional object.

I often invite patients to call in times of crisis, but always with the same boundaries I set with Debbie. Sometimes, someone might call several times between appointments. I make a point of discussing this in sessions, confirming the boundaries while acknowledging how hurtful and unfair it must feel that I'm not always available when I'm needed. What can emerge from this is the fear of even trying to tolerate anxiety or stress: a feeling that has to be "shut off" before it's fully experienced just in case it becomes too much to bear. (This partly explains why some people who self-harm can't describe any emotions preceding self-harm.)

My work with Debbie highlighted, yet again, the aggression towards and contempt of others that often lie beneath self-harming behaviour: not only did Debbie identify with her mother's view of herself as always "falling short", she turned a similar lens on to those around her. She had introjected a cruel and hypercritical voice. This was apparent in her relationship with me as well as in the hostile way in which she sometimes spoke about Steve.

Towards the end of her therapy, she attended a charity dinner and was introduced to a television personality. She spent about a quarter of her session criticising this man and his flamboyant manner in the most contemptuous terms. I suggested gently to her that she was turning on him the unkind attacks she'd experienced from her mother. Debbie looked at me blankly: she struggled to see her own aggression, and this was one area that we hadn't really addressed during our work together. She still wasn't able to "own" her anger as something healthy and helpful; she may not have been using it so often against herself but, at times, she was using it to express towards others that she once expressed against herself.

Often, Debbie channelled her aggression into humour. Initially, her humour was generally designed to minimise her feelings and experiences or undermine herself. Eventually, she developed a somewhat satiric edge that while sometimes unkind was generally accurate, dry and with the comic timing that many stand-ups would have envied. A supervisor once told me that a therapist should never laugh at a patient's jokes in case they camouflaged a more serious point. With Debbie, I threw this guidance out of the window: not to have laughed would have been persecutory. The important issue, once we'd stopped laughing, was to look at what might lie underneath the humour.

Sometimes patients come back to address the next stage in their "growth" or a new and difficult situation or relationship. I'd like to see Debbie again: despite being brought up to believe that everything about her was inadequate, she became able to value herself as a bright, funny, and interesting woman. I only hope that should she ever consider a return to psychotherapy, it will be to continue her work rather than because she's felt the need to return to self-harm.

References

Bion, W. R. (1959). Attacks on linking. *International Journal of Psycho-Analysis, 40*: 308–315.

Bowlby, J. (1988). *A Secure Base*. Abingdon: Routledge.

Green, A. (1986). The dead mother. (K. Aubertin, Trans.) In: *On Private Madness* (pp. 142–173). London: Karnac. (Reprinted London: Karnac, 1997).

Greenwood, L. (2009). Absences, transitions and endings: threats to successful treatment. In: A. Motz (Ed.), *Managing Self-Harm: Psychological Perspectives* (pp. 142–156). Hove: Routledge.

Lacey, J. H., & Evans, C. D. H. (1986). The impulsivist: a multi-impulsive personality disorder. *British Journal of Addiction, 81*: 641–649.

Williams, G. (1997). The "no-entry system" of defences. In: G. Williams (Ed.), *Internal Landscapes and Foreign Bodies: Eating Disorders and other Pathologies* (pp. 115–122). London: Duckworth.

Winnicott, D. W. (1960). Ego Distortion in Terms of True and False Self. In: *The Maturational Process and the Facilitating Environment* (pp. 140–152). London: Hogarth. (Reprinted London: Hogarth, 1965).

CHAPTER SIX

Using "intent" to remedy mal-attachment

Bob Johnson

I first worked in a unit for drug addicts in New York state as a senior psychiatrist in 1965. I was struck then by the behaviour patterns that are so prevalent in this group of clients. In the forty-eight years since, I have been deeply impressed by two things, first, that addiction takes an infinite number of forms limited only by the human imagination. Thus we have addictions to any human activity you care to name; sex, hobbies, money, work, violence, and stalking, together with the more conventional ones of gambling, alcohol, nicotine, legal, and illegal drugs.

Second, every addict I have met, especially those in Parkhurst Prison, has made what appears to be a choice to bury themselves in the addiction, to persist in what everyone else can see as self-destructive behaviour, driven there by severe and heavily obscured emotional pain. If the addict once desists, they are terrified that the emotional pain that they fear so much will overwhelm them so they continue their addiction, whatever it might be, as if their life depended on it, which, as they see it, it does. The roots of this "long term suicide" are to be found in their earliest mal-attachments, just as Bowlby saw with such clarity in his concept of how insecure attachment patterns develop from early relational misattunement and trauma. The term mal-attachment I use as shorthand for where the original attachment bond is less than sound. The remedy, across the board, is to prove to the person's satisfaction that adult interdependence is vastly superior to any residues of infantile dependence, not always easy to secure, but infinitely fruitful when it is.

Bowlby's inspiration was to see the crucial relevance of attachment between infant and caregiver from birth onwards. In my presentations I always show a video clip of a newborn infant responding to a social "conversation" with his father, within seventeen minutes of birth. I insist on showing this video clip wherever I'm asked to speak. Not only does it confirm Bowlby's acute insight but it counters the misinformed notion that babies cannot see, cannot reason, and can safely be treated as "lumps of wood".

Another slide I invariably show is the front cover of the *Sunday Times Magazine*, dated 22 June 2003. This depicts five newborn infants sleeping innocently and soundly in their cots, while the labels attached to them read, "SMOKER, ALCOHOLIC, SEX ADDICT, VIOLENT CRIMINAL, DRUGS USER." The caption reads "BIRTH DEFECTS—Since addiction was found to be an inherited disease, science has sought an effective cure. How close are we to eradicating society's most virulent illness?"

I find it difficult to express the depth of my personal repugnance at this statement, and indeed at the whole inhumane stance behind it. I scrawl "sacrilege", in large letters across it, but this is paltry compared with what I really think. All mental health problems, especially and including addiction, are "software problems", not "hardware problems" and require copious software support and insight to correct. In fact, as the following assorted case histories show, the problems are remarkably similar whatever the presentation.

Accordingly, I have no difficulty in stating that the answer to the question in the title of the conference is unequivocally that "Broken Bonds DO lead to addictive behaviours". The key concept behind this approach is, following Bowlby, the fact that childhood attachment matters. Since Bowlby's time, we have had Alice Miller (1987), who correctly stated the importance to us as adults of attuned early attachment relationships:

> I don't know of a single person who enjoyed this respect as a child and then as an adult had the need to put other human beings to death. (Miller, 1987, p. 177)

I was uncertain about this before I worked with sixty murderers in Parkhurst Prison—I now know for a clinical fact that precisely the same also applies to addicts—addiction too is inconceivable where secure infant attachment prevailed. Conversely, once the sufferer can be convinced that a sound adult "attachment" is available, and can be secured in real life, then, and not before, this conviction becomes curative.

Here are some case examples from my work. The first indicates how fear can infest psychotic symptoms. Anita is thirty-eight and has suffered all varieties of psychoses over ten years. When pursuing her current terrors which were so clearly left over from infancy, I was struck by how smoothly she could say the words, "Mum is alive." At the time, though we all knew that her mother had died thirty years before, there was simply no way she could articulate the words "Mum is dead." Now, as she begins to do so, all her psychotic symptoms fade. This is not addiction in the ordinary sense, but it is not stretching things too far to say she was "addicted" to her mother, the attachment had been so poor, that "detachment" from this wounding relationship towards a healthy interdependence has been decidedly problematic for Anita.

Ben, aged forty-four was also afflicted with psychotic symptoms, but in his case he was also partially addicted to psychoactive drugs which, despite much encouragement from me, he is obstinately reluctant to give up. His presenting condition he describes thus; "I'm stuck at two." Later in the video clip we explore the reasons behind this curious stance—it is that adulthood is too frightening for him. He is stuck. He needs copious encouragement that he can indeed survive on his own, without either parent (one of whom is already dead), or psychoactive drugs.

Charlie is a thirty-five-year-old life sentenced prisoner. He disclosed six years ago that he had been sexually abused. When I examined him I suggested he apply my "Trauma Triad". This involves lifting your right hand and saying very clearly, "STOP". He reluctantly did this to please me. However, when I revisited him eight weeks later, he was enthusiastic. He said, "It works!" He told me his nightmares were receding, his flashbacks fading and he was socialising better. On the first occasion we met I had suggested he imagined seating his abuser in the empty chair. He assured me that if he was sitting there he would kill him, a promise I had no reason to disbelieve. On the second occasion I ventured to repeat this suggestion. "Oh, don't bother with him", he said. From murderous intent, to confirmed indifference, how many more lives could be saved by engaging with people this way?

Daphne was a nineteen-year-old asylum seeker who had been "sex-trafficked". In my work with her I needed a translator since she only spoke Somali. Accordingly I reinforced my trauma therapy approach by asking her to hold her hand up, as with Charlie. She did so reluctantly at first. On follow-up she too was ecstatic. The corrosive symptoms of Post-Traumatic Stress Disorder (PTSD) had gone, she was socialising again, studying successfully and generally happier.

Emily, a psychotherapist in her mid forties, who had been abused and was currently contemplating suicide every few hours. After four sessions she revealed that aged thirteen, her stepfather had had his hands round her throat, throttling her while her mother stood by. Since my aim is to bring these traumas into the present, so they can be disposed of, I suggested that her stepfather (who in fact had died twenty years ago) was outside the door and was about to come in. She didn't look at the door, but at me. "You'll be here?", she asked urgently. I assured her I would sock it to any ghost that happened my way. Her suicidality evaporated. (Please note this may sound simple but it is complex, so do not try it without adequate support and supervision. In my experience re-traumatisation is a constant and potentially lethal risk).

The most recent individual with an addiction with whom I have worked is Florrie, aged forty-six. Her addiction was not to any drug or activity but to another person whom she was engaged in compulsively stalking. Her "mal-attachment" was deeply buried behind mountains of existential and other phenomenological philosophy. We slowly inched towards detaching her from her deceased father, a process which we have failed so far to complete. This email extract reveals some of the current travails she is going through:

> What I can say though, is that the pain that I have been talking about feels very real and tangible, even physically so, and that the box that seems to be opening, does not seem to be empty.
>
> There is great fear, however misplaced, huge anger at life (or even God) in general, right now specifically directed towards a certain person who has come very close to me. I now know this anger should be directed to the right source, but it is easier said than done!
>
> Moreover, before the anger, it feels as if I was fatally wounded and it is this wound I don't know what to do about. When anybody

touches this wound (and this person certainly has!) then I get very
upset and very angry indeed. It feels as if I have been handicapped
for life.

What is immediately apparent from this excerpt is the facility she has
with words. She can blend them, twirl them and conceals a great deal
behind them. This facility undoubtedly hampered our progress. However, note how clearly and how deeply she feels the pain, "very real
and tangible", a true observation and an indication of the severe mental pain that all addicts seek to cover over. She even goes so far as to
state, "I now know this anger should be directed to the right source,
but it is easier said than done!". What we have here then is a complete
intellectual grasp of the source of the pain but a severely hampered
emotional solution to it. She knows at one level that detachment from
her father is the answer but it's too painful to contemplate or enact.
Bowlby's attachment theory points to the root, her inadequate attachment relationship in childhood, unhappily I couldn't summon adequate emotional support at this time to validate her experience and
enable her to mourn this loss and so be able to thereby switch to "adult
mode".

These case histories come from a wide range of my experience. They
lead me to change the often used diagnostic label, "personality disorder" to "perception disorder." Solely because of "mal-attachment",
these adults persist in what I call being in an "infant-mode".
As described in the examples from my work, they need persuading that adult-mode is not only safer but also fully achievable, something that is vastly easier when sound attachment has been available in
the first place, as Bowlby avers. Equally, the diagnostic term "psychotic
disorder" needs replacing with "bottled-up disorder". All psychotic
symptoms, in my experience, start with a traumatic event, upon which
a whole series of other tragedies mount. By peeling them back, as with
Anita and Ben, the "mal-attachment" can be remedied, by a consistently sound and attuned adult attachment.

These conclusions have steadily become more robust over the decades. They are "simple, but not easy". In fact underlying every psychiatric symptom, whether that be anorexia, hallucinations, paranoia,
depression, bi-polar, psychosis, anxiety, panic attacks, addictions, violence, criminality, murder, or war, is a fear, an infantile fear—the loss of
an infant parental attachment bond. In fact, this approach can be tabu-
lated as follows—

Disease comparisons

1	Disease	Cholera	Perception disorder/emotional distress
2	Pathogen	Cholera germ	Fear
3	Antidote	Sanitation	Trust—healing hand of kindness
4	Lesion/pathology	Gut rot	Infantism = infant emotions in adulthood
5	Remove cause >> 100% CURE		

Row 1 gives the label attached to the disease. Take cholera first. We now know for certain that the pathogen is the cholera germ, that cholera cannot occur while the sanitation is intact and that the lesion, often fatal, is gut disorder. Note that this explanation was simply not available prior to microscopes. Indeed a prominent Berlin pathologist killed himself when his opposition to the "Germ theory" was dramatically undermined.

Following down the right-hand column, the pathogen I find for all varieties of psychiatric disorder, especially including addiction, is a profound fear, essentially a terror. This terror is hidden to start with, for safe keeping, but removable given adequate resources. The antidote is trustworthy emotional support as in the healing hand of kindness as part of a therapeutic relationship. The lesion or pathology is "infantism", my term for the situation where infant survival strategies are continued into adult life, as in the case of Fiona described above. Infantism is a novel term for an elementary process—where attachment in infancy is unsound, and insecure, then that person once they do arrive in adulthood is deprived of the chance to update his survival strategies.

The conclusion I draw from this analogy is that since we now know that cholera can be eliminated, it follows that we can also eliminate irrationality and all associated psychiatric symptoms. I concede that not too many follow this simple but not easy plan, but I have to say that when I do, I find the clinical rewards to be overwhelming.

For completion, I included the triad of "truth, trust & consent", where truth is what is really out there, trust is the antidote to fear, because you come to rely on another's truth, while consent empowers.

In concluding this brief account of my presentation to this excellent conference, I would refer back to the sacrilege that currently passes for the rationale for much psychiatric and psychological thinking today. The notion that "addiction was found to be an inherited disease" is anathema to me, especially as it feeds the nihilism that currently prevails and blocks the ineffable blossoming which occurs when a more humane attachment informed model, is implemented.

Reference

Miller, A. (1980). *For Your Own Good*. London: Virago.

CHAPTER SEVEN

Struggling with abstinence

Richard Gill

When I first saw the title of the conference, "Do broken bonds and early trauma lead to addictive behaviours?", I thought yes, of course they do, end of story. But does just the knowledge of broken bonds and early trauma help a person to stop an addiction? I thought no, not in my experience, only indirectly, there is too much history in the way. I hope I can go some way in this chapter to explain this, describe where a chemically dependent person is at when thinking of stopping and what is needed for recovery.

I begin by quoting from Flores (2004), to outline some of the underlying basis of my understanding of the links between our attachment needs and addiction and then expand on this with my experience of working with people with various forms of addiction.

> John Bowlby saw the need for healthy relationships that provide mutual affect regulation as an integral part of human behaviour from the "cradle to the grave". Kohut agreed, and said that we never outgrow our need for self objects, and that therapy is only complete when the person can form healthy attachments outside the therapeutic milieu. Another very important aspect of attachment theory and self psychology is their compatibility with the fellowship of AA

(Alcoholics Anonymous). Kohut viewed the narcissistic disorder as the expression of a reaction to injury of the self, and regarded the experience of the bond between the self and the self object to be crucial for psychological health and growth, Kohut is implying that there is an inverse relationship between individual's early experience of the positive self object responsiveness and their propensity to turn to alcohol, drugs and other sources of gratification as substitutes for these missing or damaging relationships.

AA and other twelve step programmes accomplish this in a number of ways. First and foremost, AA provides a predictable and consistent holding environment that allow addicts and alcoholics to have their self object needs met in a way that is not exploitative, destructive, or shameful. Because of unmet developmental needs addicts and alcoholics have such a strong and overpowering need for human responsiveness that they feel insatiable and shamed by their neediness. Through their identification with other alcoholics and addicts, they come to accept in themselves what they could not accept previously because they believed their badness was unique. (Flores, 2004, pp. 96–97)

I suppose the presumption in the conference was that abstinence is desirable, so that someone who has suffered from an addiction cannot only come to live with how he feels but also to enjoy how he feels drug free. Abstinent, certainly for long enough, to enable a person to learn enough about themselves to be able to take from life that which makes life meaningful and fulfilling. However, with chemical addiction, how long this period is, is open to debate. Why would someone want to go back to using a substance that could re-establish a life threatening addiction anyway? My contribution is focused on alcohol and drugs, although the recovery from these takes a similar path to other addictions that have different identities and circumstances.

The motivation for any addiction is fear and by the time a person approaches stopping their use (of alcohol or drugs), that fear includes terror as well. Fear of the circumstances that have resulted from their using and drinking and the terror of who they may become if they stop the addiction.

As has been shown so far by the other contributors, a great deal is known today about the cause and science of addictions but to the person who is an addict (referring to someone that is addicted to alcohol as well) this is of little help as such, the only neural pathway it has opened up is one that has led to all that is negative in life, creating a rigid defensive structure. The person with an addiction is lost in the terror of what he thinks reality is. In the late 1950s Michael Balint (1957) explored in his book called *The Basic Fault* the state of schizophrenia and pathological narcissism by describing the mental decline of an alcoholic. Although we can now safely look at addiction as having its foundation in broken attachments and early trauma, we also know that addiction does have a life of its own and is a trauma in itself. So when working with addiction, both the trauma and the reality of the consequences of the trauma need to be worked with. As Thomas Merton (2005, p. XII) wrote in *No Man Is An Island*,

> In the last analysis, the individual is responsible for living his own life and for finding himself. If he persists in shifting his responsibility to someone else, he fails to find out the meaning of his existence. (Merton, 2005, p. XII)

The past reality of the consequences of trauma is dark for the addict but through his addiction it is encased in denial, shame, and guilt. We are looking here today at how these traumas need to be dealt with.

My experience is that for most people with an addiction early trauma and the derailment experienced from their original attachment relationships and the patterns that emerge take a few years to surface to consciousness. Hopefully it is the repetitions of these early traumas that can be looked at and worked with in a therapeutic relationship.

So what does the person with an addiction need when the decision to stop using has been made. She is in effect making the painful choice to say goodbye to a loved one, a main carer, a partner depended upon for rescue from all difficult situations. The person is beginning to realise how they operate in life just doesn't work anymore but is however reluctant to admit that any of their failures are down to them, it is more often than not the other who is at fault. Shame and guilt prevent exploration and denial is their main defense. Dismissive or preoccupied attachment patterns are easy to recognise whilst many could be seen to have a more disorganised and unresolved pattern of behaviour and thinking. What helps at this stage is to separate out the person from the substance whilst the therapist holds, or is at least aware of, the other dynamics. For example the train driver who is travelling 160 miles a day to attend therapy and struggling with the question "Has your drinking ever endangered someone's life?" He finds himself insisting on talking about his constipation or his car that won't work rather than face the painful realities. Then after four weeks bursts into my room one morning and says "Driving a train whilst drinking does endanger lives doesn't it Richard?" I never heard about his bowels or car again.

Then there is the example of a woman who resentfully talks about having just been caught on CCTV in a compromising activity at work, when asked the question "Would you have done that if you weren't drinking?" breaks down with the realisation that it was only because she was drinking that it happened at all. This separation of the person from the substance is received with relief and is the start of dissolving the shame that binds all the other defenses together. I suggest, as Jason Wright has stated in his chapter (which opened the conference), that people with an addiction need a community, a group of people that at a core level understand. When I was working at SHARP (the Self Help Addiction Recovery Programme, a five day a week three month outpatient programme which I designed and ran for five years in London), I didn't know then that Jason was running the CORE programme at the other end of the same borough. The content of the programmes were in detail different but the overall containing psychodynamic structure, group content and emphasis on abstinence were the same, so I won't repeat what Jason has already described in his chapter. However, I do need to emphasise here the necessity, in my view, for the influence and power of the group to facilitate early recovery and the ongoing need for community to maintain life long stability.

The SHARP programme did have a content that other more scientific and psychodynamically based programmes have not, and that was the base of the "twelve steps" of Alcoholics Anonymous (AA). An underpinning that provides ongoing containment and a way of breaking through the denial around addiction, whether that be chemical or behavioural. I sometimes think that we as therapists at SHARP had it easier than the therapists at CORE. Why you might ask? Well, when someone decides to stop an addiction they want something simple, a structure to hang on to. Apart from the obvious answer to "How do I not use?", that is, "stop using", they still want to know how. Whilst in treatment the first prerequisite is the need to get there, which is a good fifty per cent of the answer. Then there is the simple guide as in step one of the AA programme (1957), "We admitted we were powerless of our addiction and that our lives were unmanageable." Why admit powerlessness?, because that allows a choice to be made. This is hard whilst denial of what chemicals have allowed a person to do is still so tightly embedded in their body and sense of who they are. So separating out the chemical from the person by examining the unmanageable consequences of using, helps clarify the choices that can be made. This is painful to do but then there are others in treatment to encourage and share with, to illuminate the benefit this process has been to them and slowly that person will see that they can make a choice as to whether they want to continue or relapse.

This of course opens up the void that they have been in terror of and many people feel that this is too much. Who wants to admit the basic truth that at the end of the day we are all powerless? Powerless over people, places, and things, the terror of powerlessness that somewhere we harbour in our psyche a fear that takes us back to early embodied memories of babyhood. We all struggle with this and make the best job of life while we are alive. However for the person with an addiction, who has been living a slow death for many years whilst having his primary relationship with a dead object, some benign concept has to enter his life. As the strapline to Dr Khantzian's book proclaims, that concept is hope, as in "hope behind the pain". The hope that is carried by the other people in the community who are further into the programme and have a little more strength and clarity. This is step two of AA (1957), "Came to believe that a power greater than ourselves could restore us to sanity". This hope starts to filter through as slowly more sense is made of the effects of chemicals in their life and their feelings are waking up and being contained rather that denied.

After about six weeks of working through these stages participants would be asked to look at and compile a list of everyone they had been hurt by, everyone they were still angry with, or those to whom they still felt resentful. Alongside this they were asked to identify how they felt and what attitude they had adopted to deal with the resentment, an attitude that would often reflect their primary defensive structures. This was a major piece of work which helped people to be more aware of their feelings and how they dealt with them. This was often a difficult time and hopefully participants had learned to be able to ask for help and gain support from the community, an action most people with an addiction find hard to take. This was step four of AA (1957), "Made a searching and fearless moral inventory of ourselves" Why do this?

Basically to find clarity about how their lives had been whilst living chemically dependently and to help them get in touch with feelings that had been denied and to identify the repetitious nature of their interactions with others. This allowed participants to start to see that their main drive was in fact to connect with others but they had not been able to thus causing so much suffering to themselves and others.

As I have said, this was a painful time but the relief came in step five of AA (1957), which is, "Admitted to God, to ourselves and another human being the exact nature of our wrongs". Archaic words but powerful, as when this step was shared with the therapist the relief was overwhelming. Shame started to fall away as their darkest secrets were exposed but not judged, feelings became bearable without resorting to using and a different acceptance of self was realised to allow a less defensive attitude towards the world in general.

Whilst all this individual work was being carried out by the clients the staff were well aware of the other difficulties people were suffering, such as eating problems, manic depression, family difficulties, sexual addiction and broken attachments. Groups were run with these issues as a focus so that family sessions could take place and relationships looked at. These groups were there in order to signpost the other difficulties they may face during their recovery, issues that hopefully they would be aware of so that relapse to chemical usage would not happen and may be dealt with by ongoing therapy. My experience was that these difficulties would only surface well after treatment had finished and may be only when their lives were more stable. In fact it is noted that it is at this safer stage in recovery when relapse is most likely to happen. That is when the earlier traumas and feelings of broken attachments surface and the associated feelings are not understood. Depression, low mood, confusion, and low self-esteem combine with the other difficulties of life, like, failure in relationships, work or the reliance on a behavioural addiction they had previously been in denial about.

It is here that many people seek out therapy and hopefully the therapist may understand the powerful therapeutic process of the "Twelve Step" movement, as often this person will still be involved in the fellowships. The community is just as important for this phase as previously and there are established groups for eating difficulties, sexual addiction, families of addicted people, adult children of alcoholics, where low self-esteem may lead to being in debt, under earning, or gambling. Here again, as in AA, the only requirement for attendance is a desire to recover from the addiction. There is no "must" anywhere in the process only a gradual journey through the other steps of recovery. Unfortunately there is no space here to expand on these.

This journey in the Anonymous Fellowships, in my experience, helps the person into a healthier life that does contain the principles inherent in healthy attachments, such as humility, open-mindedness, patience, compassion, courage, and forgiveness where appropriate. Through the narratives of people's lives that are openly shared in all the fellowships, identification is again made, that gives permission for someone to be vulnerable instead of ashamed of their life's actions.

Anyone can attend an open meeting and it saddens me when I hear that people in their ignorance of the Anonymous Fellowships term a spiritual programme "religious". When I think of the fact that the main principles for healthy attachment are proximity and attunement and that in London alone there are over 900 meetings of AA and NA (Narcotics Anonymous) every week, attended by at least 10,000 people where a person in recovery can go, be understood and supported.

As Jason Wright has described in his chapter, addiction in society today is not the problem, it is how addiction is seen and what causes addiction to manifest that needs to be understood. The same with the person with an addiction and how therapy, in conjunction with the twelve step programme or other recovering communities, can allow that pain carried by the individual, to be understood and released, that leads to a more fulfilled life and a more tolerant society.

References

Alcoholics Anonymous. (1953). *Twelve Steps and Twelve Traditions*. New York: AA World Service.

Balint, M. (1957). *The Basic Fault*. London: Routledge.

Flores, P. J. (2004). *Addiction as an Attachment Disorder*. New York: Jason Aronson.

Khantzian, E. J., & Albanese, J. (2008). *Understanding Addiction as Self Medication*. Lanham, MD: Rowman & Littlefield.

Merton, T. (1955). *No Man Is An Island*. New York: Houghton Mifflin Harcourt.

CHAPTER EIGHT

Technology, attachment, and sexual addiction

Cara Crossan

Introduction

Since the 1980s, sexually addictive behaviour has received an increased amount of attention with some arguing that this disorder should either be classified as sexual compulsion, hypersexuality or problematic sexual behaviour (Giugliano, 2006; Gold & Hefner, 1998; Goodman, 1998). Amongst clinicians, there appears to be a lack of consensus when writing about this topic. There has been a great deal of controversy regarding how we define sexual addiction with the definition differing between articles. Authors such as Kalichman and Rompa (2001), and Quadland (1985) have changed the definition several times throughout their papers. The lack of research supporting any one particular theory or concept has helped explain why some clinicians have used the terms interchangeably (Giugliano, 2006; Gold & Hefner, 1998; Hook, Hook & Hines, 2008; Lloyd, Raymond, Miner & Coleman, 2007).

The internet has changed the face of sexual addiction and how clients are presenting for treatment.

- "Sex" continues to be the most frequently searched term on the internet (Freeman-Longo & Blanchard, 1998; Cooper, McLoughlin, & Campbell, 2000; Putnam, 2000).
- Every second somewhere around the world, around 30,000 cyber users are viewing pornography online (Top Ten Reviews, 2009).
- Internet dependent users gradually spent less time with real people in their lives in exchange for solitary time in front of a computer (Shotton, 1991).
- Sexual activity no longer requires physical contact.
- Studies of internet addicts found that fifty-three per cent of serious relationship problems were due to cyber affairs and online sexual compulsivity (Young, 1998a).
- Cooper, Delmonico and Burg (2000) claim that as internet usage continues to increase we may experience an explosion of clients presenting for sex addiction.

The availability, accessibility, convenience, affordability and anonymity of stimulating content can contribute to highly addictive behaviour or experience (Cooper, 1998). Although technologies and the internet can be used for healthy sexual expression and for relationships, it can also give rise to significant problems (Cooper, Delmonico & Burg, 2000).

Copper (1998) clearly explains why he believes online sexual addiction has been exacerbated by technology and access to the internet, calling it the three A's of cybersex: Anonymity, Accessibility, and Affordability.

- **Anonymity**: provides the user with a sense of perceived control over the content, tone, and nature of the online experience. It allows the internet user to secretly engage in erotic behaviours without the fear of being caught. People with pre-existing social, emotional issues (shy, avoidant, rejection sensitive etc.) no longer need to evolve a social skill set in order to meet people, have sex, make friends or be soothed.
- **Accessibility**: Most mobile devices are internet enabled, allowing for twenty-four hours a day, seven days a week access and the barrier to most websites with "adult material", is an easily bypassed age restriction.
- **Affordability**: Viewing or seeking sexual partners no longer costs money. Increasing accessibility through personal gadgets means certain behaviours are easier to hide.

Increasing numbers of clients and their partners are seeking treatment for excessive porn use, anonymous sex, and prostitution with many spending inordinate amounts of time on social networking sites. Greenfield (1999) noted that online sexual behaviour often progresses from virtual, to actual sex.

Social networking sites have made use of technology to provide its client base with mobile access. GRINDR, a "geosocial networking application geared towards gay, bisexual, and bi-curious men", has 3,000 new users a day, with users logging on approximately eight times per day and spending an average of 1.3 hours using the app. The application now has versions in 180 countries around the world (PR Newswire, 2010).

There are different theories about why people become sex addicted. Carnes is probably the most prolific writer on this topic and has been credited with naming this problem "sexual addiction". Carnes believes its origin is rooted in early, developmental attachment failure with the primary caregivers (Carnes, 1983, 1991; Schwartz, & Brasted, 1996). By understanding the implications of early attachment between infant and primary caregiver we may get closer to the origins of sexual addiction (Brennan & Shaver, 1995).

Bowlby (1977) viewed attachment as a strong affectional bond between the primary caregiver and the child. Attachment patterns have to do with how the infant is tended to by the primary caregiver. There are four attachment patterns:

The **secure attachment pattern** is a healthy, secure bond that is formed in early childhood when the caregiver responds to the child's needs (Bowlby, 1977). The secure attachment pattern gives rise to a person who is comfortable showing love and affection to their loved one and equally comfortable being alone and independent. They do not require a relationship to make them feel happy or complete (Adams, 2011). How they become attached to others is a result of the kind of attachment relationship they had with their primary caregivers (Ainsworth, Blehar, Waters & Wall, 1978).

An **insecure bond** is formed when the caregiver is neglectful of the child's needs or emotionally dysregulated (i.e., depressed, anxious, fearful). Insecure attachments give rise to people presenting with an inability to emotionally attach known as the love avoidance, or emotional anorexia (Adams, 2011).

Anxiously attached men and woman exhibit very high levels of love obsession, when compared to those with other attachment patterns

(Stephen & Bachman, 1999). Those with anxious and avoidant patterns desire more sexual partners compared to those with a secure attachment pattern (Miller & Fishkin, 1997). Katehakis (2009) found that an avoidant attachment pattern often accompanied sexual addiction, whilst Carnes (1991) found that seventy-eight per cent of 204 sex addicts came from disengaged or avoidant families; and Schwartz and Brasted (1995) have been examining sexual addiction as an aspect of Post-Traumatic Stress Disorder and dissociative disorders.

Summary

Working with clients who have a sex addiction is as complex as the addiction itself. Carnes believes by breaking the secrecy and shame of the addiction, recovery is possible.

People with addictions—regardless of the nature of the addiction—are typically dysregulated (Adams, 2011). They are seeking relief from underlying issues like emotional pain, depression, or anxiety. People with a sexual addiction have learned to either escape or avoid strong feelings through the addictive use of sexual behaviour and, often, multiple addictions (Carnes, 1989).

Various studies have explored how negative affects such as shame could be a precursor to sexual addiction. Baumeister (2003) emphasises the importance of self-regulation, a failure to internalise self soothing strategies could be a precursor to addictive behaviour.

Sexual addiction is an addiction and it is very important to look beyond the client's sexual behaviours when addressing their therapeutic options and recovery and an integrated therapeutic approach needs to be considered. Research has shown that twelve step programmes such as Sex and Love Addicts Anonymous (SLAA) and relapse prevention groups are effective strategies for treating sexual addiction (Adams & Robinson, 2001; Graham & Glickhauf-Hughes, 1992). Several authors also suggest treatment should also include individual psychotherapy, gender specific therapeutic groups, and relapse prevention (Adams & Robinson, 2001; Carnes, 2001; Goodman, 1998; Katehakis, 2009).

Case study

Michael was in his twenties, a good-looking, single, body conscious, fit, and popular guy. He is an only child and has lived a comfortable life. However, he was living a part of his life in secret: he was a cybersex addict, and his thirst for internet pornography and anonymous sex was uncontrollable.

Michael's earliest childhood memories included daily masturbation and viewing sexually explicit images, found tucked away in boxes in his father's garage. He described his father as being aloof and absent, often working away from home. Later, colleagues of Michael's father would describe him as being a ladies man and bragging about his father's VIP status at strip clubs and the like. From this, Michael learned that sexual conquests and anonymous sex were seen as manly and heroic.

Michael's mother was a model and came from a family of secrets. Her childhood was turbulent and she was sexually abused for many years. She was chronically dysregulated. Michael grew up experiencing his mother as depressed, anxious, and unavailable to him.

Michael was offered weekly one to one therapy, a male recovery group and the recommendation that he attend a twelve-step fellowship. Michael revealed that as a young adult, he had been in a turbulent relationship and he had remained in that relationship for three years, despite the emotional abuse he experienced. Michael was constantly belittled by his partner, for failing to satisfy her, and he came to experience sex as shameful. After their break up, Michael became afraid of and avoided, intimacy.

Michael came to realise that he had not experienced appropriate input and modelling from his parents and that he had turned to substances and sexual behaviours to find temporary relief from his own internal dysregulation. Michael recognises his avoidant attachment pattern developed in infancy, when some of his basic care and emotional needs were neglected—his mother would avoid physical contact with him after a certain age. Later in therapy, it was revealed that she feared that such contact would be seen as unhealthy and akin to sexual abuse. Parker and Guest (2003) suggest that when there is a failure to internalise soothing behaviours during childhood, addictive behaviour might become the primary method of affect regulation.

References

Adams, K. M. (2011). *Silently Seduced: When Parents Make their Children Partners, Understanding Covert Incest*. Deerfield Beach, FL: Health Communications.

Adams, K. M., & Morgan, A. P. (2007). *When he's Married to Mom: How to Help Mother Enmeshed Men Open their Hearts to True Love and Commitment.* New York, NY: Fireside Books.

Adams, K. M., & Robinson, D. W. (2001). Shame reduction, affect regulation, and sexual boundary development: Essential building blocks of sexual addiction. *Sexual Addiction & Compulsivity, 8:* (1), 23–44.

Ainsworth, M., Blehar, M., Waters, E., & Wall, S. (1978). *Patterns of Attachment: Assessed in the Strange Situation and at Home.* Hillsdale, NJ: Erlbaum.

Barbarin, O. A., & Tirado, M. (1985). Enmeshment, family processes, and successful treatment of obesity. *Family Relations, 34:* 115–121.

Baumeister, R. F. (2003). Ego depletion and self-regulation failure: A resource model of self-control. *Alcoholism: Clinical and Experimental Research, 27,* (2): 281–284.

Bowlby, J. (1958). The nature of the child's tie to his mother. *International Journal of Psychoanalysis, 39:* 350–373.

Bowlby, J. (1977). *The Making and Breaking of Affectional Bonds.* London: Tavistock.

Brady, K. (1996). Dropouts rise a net result of computers. *The Buffalo Evening News,* 21 April, p. 1.

Brennan, K. A., & Shaver, P. R. (1995). Dimensions of adult attachment, affect regulation, and romantic relationship functioning. *Society for Personality and Social Psychology, 21,* (3): 267–283.

Carnes, P. (1983). *The Sexual Addiction.* Minneapolis, MN: Comp Care.

Carnes, P. (1991). *Don't Call it Love: Recovery from Sexual Addiction.* New York: Bantam Books.

Carnes, P. (2001). *Out of the Shadows: Understanding Sexual Addiction* (3rd edition). Center City, MN: Hazelden.

Carnes, P. J. (2002). The fire next time: Implications of changes in our understanding of human sexuality. Presentation at the National Council on Sexual Addiction and Compulsivity conference: Nashville.

Cooper, A. (1998). Sexuality and the Internet: Surfing into the new millennium. *Cyber Psychology & Behavior, 1:* 181–187.

Cooper, A., Delmonico, D., & Burg, R. (2000). Cybersex users, abusers, and compulsives: New findings and implications. In: A. Cooper (Ed.), *Cybersex: The Dark Side of the Force,* (pp. 5–29). Philadelphia: Brunner Routledge.

Cooper, A., McLoughlin, I. P., & Campbell, K. M. (2000). Sexuality in cyberspace: Update for the 21st century. *Cyber Psychology & Behavior, 3;* 521–536.

Freeman-Longo, R. E., & Blanchard, G. T. (1998). *Sexual abuse in America: Epidemic of the 21st century.* Brandon, VT: Safer Society Press.

Gavazzi, S. M., Anderson, S. A., Sabatelli, R. (1993). Family differentiation, peer differentiation, and adolescent adjustment in a clinical setting. *Journal of Adolescent Research, 8*: 205–225.

Giugliano, J. (2006). Out of control sexual behaviour: A qualitative investigation. *Sexual Addiction & Compulsivity, 13*: 361–375.

Gold, S. N., & Hefner, C. L. (1998). Sexual addiction: Many conceptions, minimal data. *Clinical Psychology Review, 18*, (3): 367–381.

Goodman, A. (1998). *Sexual Addiction.* Madison, CT: International Universities Press.

Graham, A., & Glickauf-Hughes, C. (1992). Object relations and addictions: The role of "transmuting externalizations". *Journal of Contemporary Psychotherapy, 22*, (1): 21–33.

Greenfield, D. N. (1999). Psychological characteristics of compulsive internet use: a preliminary analysis. *Cyber Psychology and Behavior, 2*, (5): 403–412.

Griffin-Shelley, E. (1991). *Sex and Love: Addiction, Treatment, and Recovery.* New York: Praeger.

Hook, J. N., Hook, J. P., & Hines, S. (2008). Reach out or act out: Long-term group therapy for sexual addiction. *Sexual Addiction & Compulsivity, 15*: 217–232.

Kalichman, S. C., & Rompa, D. (2001). The sexual compulsivity scale: Further development and use with HIV-Positive persons. *Journal of Personality Assessment, 76*, (3): 379–395.

Katehakis, A. (2009). Affective neuroscience and the treatment of sexual addiction. *Sexual Addiction & Compulsivity, 16*: 1–31.

Kinnier, R. T., Brigman, S. L. & Noble, F. C. (1990). Career indecision and family enmeshment. *Journal of Counselling & Development, 68*: 309–312.

Lloyd, M., Raymond, N. C., Miner, M. H., & Coleman, E. (2007). Borderline personality traits in individuals with compulsive sexual behaviour. *Sexual Addiction & Compulsivity, 14*, (3): 187–206.

Miller, L. C. & Fishkin, S. A. (1997). On the dynamics of human bonding and reproductive success: Seeking windows on the adapted-for-human-environmental interface. In: J. A. Simpson & D. T. Kenrick (Eds.), *Evolutionary Social Psychology* (pp. 197–235). Mahwah, NJ: Lawrence Erlbaum.

Parker, J., & Guest, D. (2003). Individualized sexual addiction treatment: A developmental perspective. *Sexual Addiction & Compulsivity, 10*: 13–22.

PR Newswire. (2010). Grindr grows to over one million members in 180 countries. Published 21 September 2010.

Putnam, R. D. (2000). *Bowling Alone: The Collapse and Revival of American Community.* New York: Simon & Schuster.

Quadland, M. C. (1985). Compulsive sexual behaviour: Definition of a problem and an approach to treatment. *Journal of Sex and Marital Therapy, 11*: 121–132.

Schwartz, M. F. (1996). Reenactments related to bonding and hypersexuality. *Sexual Addiction & Compulsivity: The Journal of Treatment & Prevention, 3*: 195–212.

Schwartz, M. F., & Brasted, W. S. (1985). Sexual addiction: Self hatred, guilt, and passive rage contribute to this deviant behavior. *Medical Aspects of Human Sexuality, 19*, (10): 103–107.

Shotton, M. (1991). The costs and benefits of "computer addiction". *Behavior and Information Technology, 10*, (3): 219–230.

Stephan, C. W., & Bachman, G. F. (1999). What's sex got to do with it? Attachment, love schemas, and sexuality. *Personal Relationships, 6*: 111–123.

Top Ten Reviews. (2009). Internet pornography statistics. Retrieved 30 August 2009.

Williams, L. M., & Hiebert, W. J. (2001). Challenging the belief system behind enmeshment. *Journal of Clinical Activities, 1*, (2): 17–28.

Young, K. S. (1998a). Internet addiction: The emergence of a new clinical disorder. *Cyber Psychology and Behavior, 1*, (3): 237–244.

Young, M. B. (1991). Attending to the shame: Working with addicted populations. *Contemporary Family Therapy, 13*, (5): 497–505.

CHAPTER NINE

Gambling addiction: seeking certainty when relationship is the risk

Liz Karter

This group is not like Gamblers Anonymous, this group is scarier
… it's like family.

—Carla, *aged forty-nine, a slot machine player*

Her statement, for that is what it was, was made solemnly with a depth of meaning and feeling by a woman with a long-term history of cross addiction, beginning with alcohol, moving on through crack cocaine, moving onto addiction to slot machine playing. To this woman—as to many men and women—by far the hardest addiction to overcome is that of gambling addiction. For the woman I speak of her pattern of addiction lasting over twenty-five years becoming ultimately so destructive it resulted in five of her eleven children being taken into care.

So, if we are honest with ourselves, what do we see when initially we visualise this woman Carla? Perhaps we see a chaotic and irresponsible woman, who certainly is old enough to know better? What I came to see as both Carla's one to one and women's group therapist was a frightened child—around eleven years' old—who just happened to be in the body of an adult woman. Carla never knew her father and was abandoned by her mother at the age of eleven when she left her to be cared for by her grandmother, in her home country of Jamaica, promising she would return. She never did. Her uncle at times would be put in charge of taking care of her whilst her grandmother worked. He would take her to the cellar and sexually abuse her. Everything Carla had done from that time on made sense if seen through the perspective of the mind of that desperately lonely and scared little girl that she was. She imagined having eleven children would guarantee that she would never experience the insufferable pain and fear of loneliness again, but without the associated risks of adult interaction and relationship. The crack cocaine was used as self-medication, helping to transcend the impossibly difficult world that she did not know she was creating by having such a large family. It blocked out any memories or flashbacks of her traumatic experience of childhood sexual abuse. Similarly compulsively pushing money into a slot machine, staring at a computer screen whilst she gambled was a desperate attempt to numb her pain.

To work with people who have a gambling addiction it is vital to understand that gambling addiction is not about the money, winning lots of money, getting rich quick, or born out of greed, or naivety about the odds of winning. The money does not matter. All that matters is to buy complete absorption in the gambling activity and so play yourself away from a world that feels too scary, too painful, too risky to inhabit. Often the biggest risk of all for the woman with gambling addiction is being in an intimate relationship.

The findings of my extensive clinical practice in the area of gambling addiction since 2001 have been that gambling addiction for women is a survival strategy, a coping mechanism, an attempt to manage life's problems by suppressing feelings because there is no trusted other with whom to experience the support and relief of healthy emotional expression. The reasons for there being no trusted other often lie in experiences of early life trauma.

Over the last seven years in which I have been a women's group therapist I have found:

- Eighty-four per cent of women who have attended women's group meetings for gambling addiction (which I have facilitated) have been the survivors of child abuse and/or domestic violence.
- Seventy-four per cent of women who have attended women's groups during that time live alone or alone with children.

This makes complete sense to me that the above statistics should reflect each other so clearly. The experience of abuse in childhood, whether it has been sexual, psychological, or emotional abuse or neglect has all the same impact; that the deepest wound is to the woman's ability to trust in another person. She is unlikely to form healthy attachments and so the woman I see for gambling addiction treatment is frequently isolated, lonely, anxious, and depressed. Gambling is to her so often a replacement for the longed for but deeply feared intimate relationship.

The effect of child abuse trauma is often that development is frozen at the time at which the abuse took place. I see so often grown women, who are perhaps mothers or even high flying professionals who inwardly, psychologically, and emotionally remain childlike and unable to cope well with either their inner world of troubling thoughts and feelings or the demands and practicalities of the outer world. Both her relationship with herself and with others is undeveloped and unsatisfying. She turns to gambling when she might otherwise turn to a friend or partner to soothe her at times of feeling sad, lonely, anxious, or angry. The slot machine, the computer screen will never abandon her, never betray her trust, never judge her behaviour or punish her for what she thinks or feels. It will, most importantly of all, help her not to feel. Addiction too, however keeps her in a stasis; no chance to grow and develop a greater ability to cope with life and its ups and downs. She ultimately develops a true dependency on gambling to soothe her, like a child depends on a parent for comfort and a sense of stability and security.

Perhaps what is unique to gambling addiction is that there are physical objects to attach to. A woman who has addiction to slot machine playing might attach to a favourite machine, viewing it as "hers" and becoming greatly distressed if another person plays her machine in her presence. The object is closely associated with soothing and emotional support in the way that an okay mother might have been in childhood. Indeed gambling might even seem to be the yearned for source of childhood memories of more pleasant times. For Victoria, gambling was a strong link to memories of her mother who enjoyed playing arcade fruit machines—the mother she lost to cancer, when she was ten years old, then losing her father, when she was fourteen years of age. Her gambling addiction began when the woman I met and worked with for two years married at a young age, seeking unconsciously the stability and security she had lost along with her parents. When her husband became abusive, returning to the arcades to play fruit machines was the closest she could get to returning home for parental support. The machines blocked out her thoughts and so soothed her feelings. An occasional win might lighten the darkness of her depression for a time. Although, only for a time of course, until the loss chasing started and too much money was lost, too much time was lost. "They suck you in, those machines … it's like I'm in a bubble …" (Victoria, age forty-six years). Spiralling debts, children neglected, social service involvement, all because of her excessive gambling. Her relationship with gambling had become like that of a child with an abusive parent; the child knows that the parent hurts them terribly, but they feel they have no choice but to stay right where they are because they cannot survive in the world without them.

To experience ambivalence in the early stages of recovery from gambling addiction, as with any addiction, is normal and natural and a manifestation of a conflict between the rational and the emotional. For the woman who has decided at least in part that she needs to stop gambling the ambivalence frequently is strong. Let us remember that is because her attachment to gambling is likely to be the strongest attachment she has, and perhaps, ever had. Gambling is perceived as offering her a sense of comfort and dependability that she has perhaps sadly not experienced from any living being. She will not let go easily and cast herself adrift without at least the hope of something else that she might depend on to get her through. At this point she remains a childlike self, feeling unable to negotiate the turbulent waters of her inner and outer world alone. Yet here again is her conflict, on the one hand instinctively knowing that she cannot go through recovery alone without help and support and yet fearing that, based on her experiential evidence, alone is the only safe way of being and that help and support are not to be trusted; especially if those who had a duty of care to her in the past have betrayed her.

Engaging women in treatment for gambling addiction and maintaining the engagement is notoriously hard and often the reason lies in the fact that therapeutic treatment involves commitment to letting go of gambling and to engage in an intimate relationship with another person in the form of the therapist; to separate from something that has caused her pain and destruction but which she feels paradoxically she can depend on and to take the perceived risk of attaching to someone who might help and support. This feels terrifying to her.

As group therapist for the last seven years I have seen in action powerful transferences toward myself as group therapist and to other members of the group. Any group experience as we know replicates our earliest group experiences and of course that of our family. I have frequently found that regardless of the level of any abuse or betrayal experienced involving the father, a seemingly lesser betrayal by a mother impacts on a deeper and more lasting level. This I see resulting in the woman throughout life withdrawing from the closeness and support offered by interpersonal relationships with women, which would be likely to be of benefit to her all round health and well being. One reason why women's group therapy has proved both so challenging and so effective in recovery is that the woman is facing her fear of close relationships with others, learning that interdependency can be desirable and healthy. Finding that it is possible to trust another enough to allow boundaries within relationships to be flexible instead of rigid and to practice healthy relational skills. Separating from gambling is a hard and painful process and to know that she is not alone, that her emotional experiences are a natural part of what it is to be human will encourage her to go forward.

In order to let go of gambling we have seen how it is essential that a woman allows herself to form relationships with others. What she often fears from closeness is not only further abusive treatment, if this lies buried in her past deep beneath her gambling behaviour, but that she also fears becoming close and then the pain of rejection and/or abandonment. The excruciating emotional and psychological pain of loss. Yet, in order to face the loss of gambling from her life she has to allow herself to take that risk; to face and to tolerate that pain.

I have found that the therapist's way of being in the consulting room is at least as important a factor in treatment outcomes as any treatment model. To present oneself as a therapist, as a "real person" present in the room is valuable. Women who have suffered abuse or domestic violence are particularly vigilant and are scared by lack of transparency. They have good reason to fear the unknown and the secretive. The use of the core skills of immediacy and congruence builds trust and a strong working alliance. Another paradox is raised however, as again we see how that which she most truly desires in her deepest self is also what she most fears. That is close relationship. She needs to feel close with her therapist, to feel that here is someone who she might work with as a stepping stone in the transition from gambling to taking her place in life in the wider world. But, what if she allows herself to be close and she loses the therapist? Maybe the loss will be through rejection if she reveals aspects of herself that the therapist might be repulsed by; lies, theft, child neglect, prostitution all are frequently consequences of gambling addiction. What if the therapist gets ill and dies? What happens when therapy ends? All these fears of loss. Of experiencing the overwhelming, wash of sickening, senses reeling, stomach cramping pain of loss ...

The above description is also how she feels at the loss of gambling. Recovery from problem gambling is experienced as a deep grief, a sense of bereavement, a broken heart at the loss of a lover. Emptiness, anxiety, depression, despair, a longing for the return of the object that took away her emotional pain, only to intensify it, but even if for just a while could again take away the pain of loss, if she could re engage with it just once more. In order to healthily negotiate the separation from gambling addiction and maintain long term recovery she will need to take what is to her the biggest risk of all; the risk of truly engaging in intimate human relationship.

Reading list

Adams, K. (2011). *Silently Seduced*. Deerfield Beach, FL: Health Communications.

Alcoholics Anonymous, (1953). *Twelve Steps and Twelve Traditions*. New York: AA World Service.

Allen, J. G., Fonagy, P., & Bateman, A. W. (2008). *Mentalizing in Clinical Practice*. Washington, DC: American Psychiatric Publishing.

Balint, M. (1957). *The Basic Fault*. London: Routledge.

Bowlby, J. (1973). *Attachment and Loss: Volume 2. Separation: Anxiety and Anger*. New York: Basic Books.

Bowlby, J. (1988). *A Secure Base*. Hove: Routledge.

Carnes, P. (1997). *The Betrayal Bond*. Deerfield Beech, FL: Health Communications.

Cooper, J., & Vetere, A. (2005). *Domestic Violence and Family Safety*. Chichester: Wiley.

Dallos, R., & Vetere, A. (2005). *Researching Psychotherapy and Counselling*. Oxford: Open University Press.

Dallos, R., & Vetere, A. (2009). *Systemic Therapy and Attachment Narratives*. London: Routledge.

De Mare, P. R., Piper, R., & Thompson, S. (1991). *Koinonia: From Hate, Through Dialogue, to Culture in the Large Group*. London: Karnac.

DuPont, R. L., & Gold, M. S. (2007). Comorbidity and "Self-Medication". *Journal of Addictive Disorders. 26*, (1): 13–23.

Elias, N. (1939). *The Civilising Process, Volume1 1, The History of Manners.* New York: Urizen. (1978)

Flores, P. J. (2004). *Addiction as an Attachment Disorder.* New York: Jason Aronson.

Gerhardt, S. (2004). *Why Love Matters.* Hove: Routledge.

Green, A. (1986). *On Private Madness.* London: Karnac. (Reprinted, London: Karnac, 1997).

Greenwood, L. (2009). Absences, transitions and endings: threats to successful treatment. In: A. Motz (Ed.), *Managing Self-Harm. Psychological Perspectives* (pp. 142–156). Hove: Routledge.

Hall, P. (2013). *Understanding and Treating Sex Addiction.* Hove: Routledge.

Hillman, J. (1968). *Suicide and the Soul.* London: Hodder & Stoughton.

Hillman, J., & Moore, T. (1989). *A Blue Fire: The Essential James Hillman.* London: Routledge.

House of Commons Health Committee. (2009). Gin Craze of the 18th century, Alcohol: First Report of Session 2009–10, 10 December 2009. www. publications.parliament.uk/pa/cm200910/cmselect/cmheal151/15111. html a32 [last accessed].

Kalsched, D. (1996). *The Inner World of Trauma: Archetypal Defense of the Spirit.* London: Routledge.

Khantzian, E. J. (1985). The self-medication hypothesis of addictive disorders. *American Journal of Psychiatry, 142*: 1259–1264.

Khantzian, E. J. (1995). Self-regulation vulnerabilities in substance abusers: Treatment implications. In: S. Dowling (Ed.), *The Psychology and Treatment of Addictive Behavior* (pp. 17–41). New York: International Universities Press.

Khantzian, E. J. (1997). The self-medication hypothesis of substance use disorders: A reconsideration and recent applications. *Harvard Review of Psychiatry, 4*: 231–244.

Khantzian, E. J. (2015). Psychodynamic psychotherapy for the treatment of substance use disorders. In: N. El-Guebaly, M. Galanter, & G. Carra, (Eds.), *The Textbook of Addiction Treatment: International Perspectives.* New York: Springer.

Khantzian, E. J., & Albanese, J. (2008). *Understanding Addiction as Self Medication.* Lanham, MD: Rowman & Littlefield.

Khantzian, E. J. & Mack, J. E. (1983). Self-preservation and the care of the self: Ego instincts reconsidered. *Psychoanalytic Study of the Child, 38*: 209–232.

Khantzian, E. J. & Mack, J. E. (1989). Alcoholics Anonymous and contemporary psychodynamic theory. In: M. Galanter (Ed.), *Recent Developments in Alcoholism* (pp. 67–89). New York: Plenum.

Kohut, H. (1971). *The Analysis of the Self.* New York: International Universities Press.

Lacey, J. H. & Evans, C. D. H. (1986). The impulsivist: a multi-impulsive personality disorder. *British Journal of Addiction, 81:* 641–649.

Maslow, A. (1968). *Towards a Psychology of Being.* New York: Van Nostrand.

McGilchrist, I. (2009). *The Master and His Emissary.* London: Yale University Press.

Menninger, K. (1938). *Man Against Himself.* New York: Free Press.

Milkman, H., & Frosch, W. A. (1973). On the preferential abuse of heroin and amphetamine. *Journal of Nervous and Mental Disease, 156:* 242–248.

Nutt, D. (2011). *Drugs Without the Hot Air.* Chicago, IL: Independent Publishing Group.

Nutt, D. (2013). "Financial crisis caused by too many bankers taking cocaine" says former drugs tsar. *Telegraph,* 16 April 2013. Available at: www.telegraph.co.uk.

Reading, B. (2002). The application of Bowlby's attachment theory to the psychotherapy of the addictions. In: M. Weegmann & R. Cohen (Eds.), *The Psychodynamics of Addiction,* (pp. xviii, 178). London: Whurr.

Schore, A. (2012). *The Art and Science of Psychotherapy.* New York: Norton.

Stolorow, R. D., Brandchaft, B., & Atwood, G. E. (1995). *Psychoanalytic Treatment: An Intersubjective Approach.* London: Routledge.

Vetere, A., & Dallos, R. (2003). *Working Systemically with Families.* London: Karnac.

Vetere, A., & Dowling, E. (2005). *Narrative Therapies with Children and Their Families.* London: Routledge.

Walant, K. B. (2002). *Creating the Capacity for Attachment: Treating Addictions and the Alienated Self.* New York: Jason Aronson.

Weider, H., & Kaplan, E. (1969). Drug use in adolescents. *Psychoanalytic Study of the Child, 24:* 399–431.

Williams, G. (1997). The no-entry system of defences. In: *Internal Landscapes and Foreign Bodies* (pp. 115–122). London: Duckworth.

Winnicott, D. W. (1960). True and false self. In: *The Maturational Process and the Facilitating Environment* (pp. 140–152). London: Hogarth. (Reprinted London: Hogarth, 1965).

The Bowlby Centre

Promoting attachment and inclusion

Since 1976 The Bowlby Centre (formerly known as CAPP) has developed as an organisation committed to the practice of attachment-based psychoanalytic psychotherapy. The Bowlby Centre is a dynamic, rapidly developing charity which aims both to train attachment-based psychoanalytic psychotherapists and to deliver a psychotherapy service to those who are most marginalised and frequently excluded from long term psychotherapy.

We provide a five-year plus part-time psychotherapy training accredited by the UKCP and operate a psychotherapy referral service for the public including the low cost Blues Project. The Bowlby Centre has a wealth of experience in the fields of attachment and loss and particular expertise in working with trauma and abuse. As part of our on-going commitment to anti-discriminatory practice we offer a consultation service to the public and private sectors and are engaged in outreach and special projects working with care leavers, women experiencing violence and abuse, offenders and ex offenders, people struggling with addiction to drugs, alcohol, eating difficulties or self harm, and to individuals and groups in a wide variety of mental health settings.

We run short courses on "Attachment and Dissociation", and "The Application of Attachment Theory to Clinical Issues" including learning disabilities. The Bowlby Centre organises conferences including the annual John Bowlby Memorial Lecture, and has a series of publications which aim to further thinking and development in the field of attachment.

Bowlby Centre members participate extensively in all aspects of the field, making outstanding theoretical, research, and clinical contributions. Their cutting edge work is consistently published in leading journals and monographs.

The Bowlby Centre Values

- The Centre believes that mental distress has its origin in failed and inadequate attachment relationships in early life and is best treated in the context of a long-term human relationship.
- Attachment relationships are shaped in the real world and impacted upon by poverty, discrimination, and social inequality. The impact of the social world will be part of the therapy.
- Psychotherapy should be available to all, and from an attachment-based psychoanalytic perspective, especially those discriminated against or described as "unsuitable" for therapy.
- Psychotherapy should be provided with respect, warmth, openness, a readiness to interact and relate, and free from discrimination of any kind.
- Those who have been silenced about their experiences and survival strategies must have their reality acknowledged and not pathologised.
- The Bowlby Centre values inclusiveness, access, diversity, authenticity, and excellence. All participants in our organisation share the responsibility for anti discriminatory practice in relation to race, ethnicity, gender, sexuality, age, (dis)ability, religion, class, educational, and learning style.

Patrons
  Sir Richard Bowlby
  Dr Elaine Arnold

INDEX